GCSE
Questions and Answers

Q&A

GEOGRAPHY

Mike Clinch Examiner
Graham Woosnam Chief Examiner

SERIES EDITOR: BOB McDUELL

Letts
EDUCATIONAL

Contents

HOW TO USE THIS BOOK	1
TYPES OF EXAMINATION QUESTION	1
ASSESSMENT OBJECTIVES IN GEOGRAPHY	2
SITTING THE EXAMINATION	3

QUESTIONS AND REVISION SUMMARIES

1 The water cycle and rivers and their valleys	4
2 Coasts	8
3 Weathering and glaciation	12
4 Weather and climate	16
5 Population and resources	23
6 Settlement	26
7 Agriculture – specifically dairying	30
8 Manufacturing industry	33
9 Retailing	36
10 Tourism and leisure	40
11 Employment structures in developed and developing countries	45

ANSWERS	52

Introduction

HOW TO USE THIS BOOK

The aim of the *Questions and Answers* series is to provide you with the help required to attain the highest level of achievement in one of your most important examinations – the General Certificate of Secondary Education (GCSE) or, in Scotland, at General and Credit levels. The books are designed to help all students, up to and including A* grade at GCSE. The series relies on the premise that an experienced examiner can provide, through examination questions, sample answers and advice, the help you need to secure success. Many revision aids concentrate on providing factual information which might have to be recalled in examinations. This series, while giving factual information in an easy-to-remember form, concentrates on the other skills which need to be developed for the new GCSE examinations.

Students often find it useful to plan their revision according to some predetermined pattern, during which weaknesses can be identified and eliminated so that confidence can grow, and so the primary consideration has been to provide main principles on which study can be based.

This *Questions and Answers* guide provides:

- Easy-to-use **Revision Summaries**.
- Advice on the different types of questions.
- Information about other skills, sometimes called **Assessment Objectives**, which will be tested apart from the recall of knowledge.
- Many examples of actual questions from a range of examination boards.
- **Sample answers** to all of the questions.
- Advice from experienced Examiners.

In order to gain the most from this book it is advised that after deciding which topic to practise, you first study the relevant revision material. Each Revision summary identifies the most important factual information pertaining to that topic. You must understand this information before progress can be made.

Next, attempt the first question. Take note of the command word at the beginning of the question, how much space is allocated for the answer and how many marks are available for each section. Note that Geography questions can be long and detailed, testing a full range of skills and using a variety of resource material. Do not be tempted to look at the answer section until you have completed the question. If you do so you may cover up some of your weaknesses.

When you have completed the question, check your responses with the answer section. The answers provided are sample answers. You do not have to match every word identically. Each sample answer attempts to outline the key points.

Take note of the advice from the examiner, especially where your answer is wrong or where you have fallen short of the maximum mark for a section. The Examiner's tip may attempt to outline a strategy for approaching the answer, or may identify pitfalls that many candidates fall into, or may simply offer advice. The advice given aims to help you improve your overall performance.

Success in GCSE examinations comes from proper preparation and a positive attitude to the examination developed through a sound knowledge of facts, an understanding of principles and a practised development of skills. This book is intended to allow candidates to develop the confidence that will lead to success.

TYPES OF EXAMINATION QUESTION

All questions in Geography examinations are there for a purpose: to find out how well you can recall factual data, how well you understand their significance and whether you can use a range of geographical skills.

Introduction

Usually, a question tests the above using one particular theme or key idea from the syllabus, though sometimes, as you will discover in this book, questions may jump from one theme to another in an attempt to ensure that all parts of the syllabus are tested.

Questions can vary in their form very widely. They range from, at one extreme, **multiple choice questions** to, at the other extreme, an **open essay**-type question. In GCSE Geography most questions are of an intermediate **structured type**.

Only a few syllabuses still set multiple choice questions. This type of question tends to test factual recall or the understanding of simple facts only, and not a candidate's ability to develop and sustain an argument. Open essay-type questions are also rare at GCSE. They aim at high level qualities such as analysis, synthesis and evaluation. Thus, if they occur at GCSE it will be in the most difficult paper of a differentiated examination.

Structured questions are the norm in most GCSE examinations. Questions of this type are broken up into small parts (a), (b), (c) and sometimes (d). These three or four subquestions may be further broken down into (i), (ii), (iii) etc. Most of the questions in this book are of this kind. Each of the subquestions will have the mark allocation alongside.

Most structured GCSE Geography questions are rich in resources – maps, photographs, graphs, diagrams, newspaper extracts etc. These are there to trigger off ideas in your mind and to provide you with information that you can make use of in your responses. Hence, these questions are often referred to as data response questions. Only small parts of these questions may demand straight factual recall.

Normally, there is an incline of difficulty in these questions; that is, the question gets progressively more difficult as one proceeds through it. The early parts of the question may seek short answers of a factual nature or may test simple skills. The later parts of the question may be more searching with explanation or discussion required. In some syllabuses, the final part may concentrate on a case study that you will be expected to have made. Do not be too worried if half-way through a question you have difficulty in answering. You personally may find the final subquestion less demanding. If you are sitting the 'more difficult' paper, in a differentiated exam, you may not have the easier 'factual recall section'. You will have more of the free response-type question, which is aimed at testing your higher levels of ability.

ASSESSMENT OBJECTIVES IN GEOGRAPHY

All GCSE Geography examinations try to test (i) your factual knowledge, (ii) your understanding and (iii) your ability to use geographical skills. Although all examination groups test these objectives, the weighting of them varies a little between examination groups (for more details contact your exam board).

Factual knowledge: this demands that you recall facts specified in the syllabus and show knowledge about specified locations and themes using geographical terminology.

Understanding: this demands that you comprehend the ideas, concepts and processes listed in the syllabus and are able to **apply** them in varying contexts. It demands that you are aware of the interrelationships that exist between people's activities and their environments, that you understand the effects of the attitudes and values of the people involved in geographical issues and in the management of environments.

Skills: you must be able to use a wide range of geographical skills. These include map interpretation skills, map drawing skills, research skills, skills in using a wide range of graphs, photographic interpretation skills, skills in communicating information and IT skills, which are particularly relevant in any enquiry work you may do.

Introduction

SITTING THE EXAMINATION

There are certain fundamental features about examinations which every year are overlooked by some candidates, to their cost. So, however obvious they may appear, it will do you no harm to think about them now.

- If you are sitting a differentiated examination, i.e. an examination where you may sit a 'less difficult' or 'more difficult' paper, make sure that you receive and answer the appropriate one.

- Be aware of the nature of the paper. Are all the questions compulsory or do you have to make a choice? If they are all compulsory, you may wish to tackle the questions you feel best prepared for first, or you may like to answer the questions in order; there are no hard and fast rules.

- If there is a choice of questions to be made, it is vital that you make the choice that is right for you. Do not be lured into choosing a question because it starts with an appealing photograph and diagram or because you find the first subquestion easy. The question might change course and become very difficult for you. In short, read all the questions through carefully before you make your choice.

- Note the mark award in the margin of the question and, if included, the number of lines the examiner has allowed you to write on. This is a good guide to the depth of answer required. There is not much sense in writing at length or continuing the answer on extension pages if the question awards only one or two marks.

- Most Geography examinations encourage you to draw sketch maps or diagrams in some of your answers. Some questions actually demand it. If this is the case, ensure that you do so, otherwise you will lose marks. Bear in mind that a well drawn, labelled sketch map or diagram can state in quite a small space much more than an equal amount of writing. There are examples of sketch maps and diagrams in this book for you to study.

- In your studies in Geography you will have learned not only facts and skills but you will also have acquired a range of ideas and concepts. An examiner may wish to test your understanding of these, perhaps in a context that is unfamiliar to you. For example, you may have studied the issue of overpopulation in north-east Brazil. The examiner may use the Nile Valley or somewhere else in the world, on which to base the question. Do not let the location deter you.

- In any examination you must be aware of the pressure of time. Work out the amount of time you have for each question if you spend the same amount on each. It is natural that if you feel supremely 'on top' of one question you may wish to spend a little longer on this than the other questions – but be careful! You must leave enough time to make a worthwhile attempt at your last question. Not answering a question, or even just a sizeable part of it, can only too easily cost you a grade.

1 The water cycle and rivers and their valleys

REVISION SUMMARY

The hydrological or water cycle is the term used to describe the progession of water falling from the atmosphere to the earth as precipitation, eventually returning to the atmosphere through the processes of evaporation and transpiration. The precipitation which falls onto the land surface, and which is not evaporated, runs over the surface through rivers and back to the sea. The diagram below summarizes the water cycle.

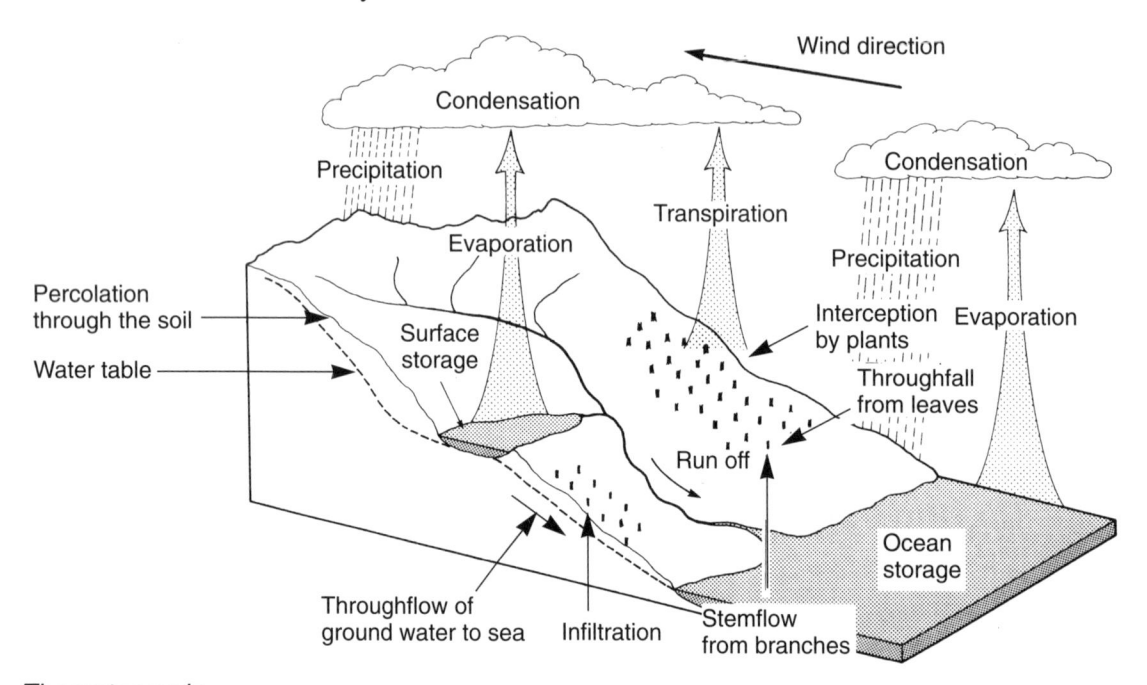

The water cycle

A **drainage basin** is an area of land drained by one river system (a river and its tributaries). The basin's limit is marked by higher land which separates it from neighbouring drainage basins. This limit is called a **watershed**.

A river system and water stored in the ground depend for their existence on precipitation. This is the drainage basin's **input**. Water moving out of the basin through the river and evaporation/transpiration is the basin's **output**. Within the basin, water may be held for a long time in lakes, the soil, vegetation and the ground. This is the basin's **storage**.

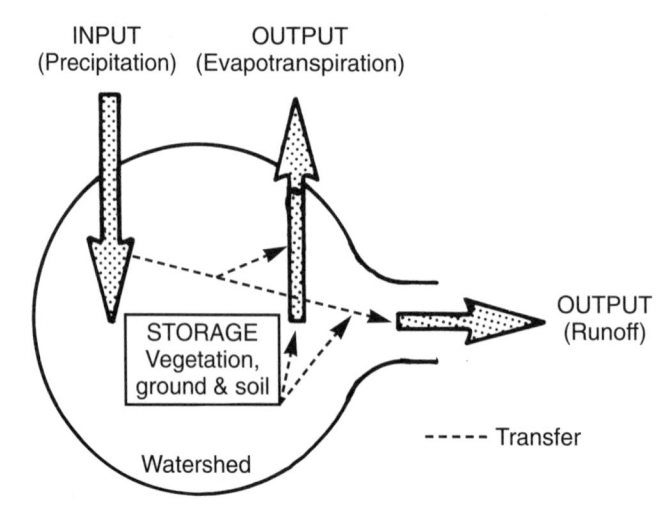

The drainage basin as a system

Rivers and streams flowing through a river basin possess energy. The amount of energy varies according to the river volume (the bigger the volume, the greater the energy), the shape of the river

The water cycle and rivers and their valleys

channel and the river gradient. This energy allows rivers to do work. They erode material from the land surface, carry this material (**load**) downstream, then deposit it in their lower courses or in the sea.

There are three main processes of erosion:

(i) **corrasion** (sometimes called abrasion) – the wearing away of the bed and banks of a river through the impacting of the river's load against them;
(ii) **hydraulic action** – the very force of water prising rocks away;
(iii) **corrosion** – the dissolving and removal in solution of some rocks, e.g. limestone, over which the river flows.

Most erosion takes place during times of flood.

LANDFORMS

The following landforms are typical of most rivers in the British Isles.

A In its upper section, a river erodes predominantly vertically so the valley will be deeper than it is wide giving a **V-shaped cross-section**. The river gradient (long profile) is steep, with **waterfalls** where it crosses rocks of different resistance, while the river's course is winding creating **interlocking spurs**.

B In its middle (valley) section the valley sides are still steep, but the valley floor is wider as the river erodes laterally as well as vertically. This flat floor (or **flood plain**) will have been created by river **meanders** as they migrate downstream. This flat land is flooded periodically. During such floods rivers deposit their load (**alluvium**), keeping the flood plain fertile.

A meander is a loop in the river's course. Water flows faster around the outside of the loop than on the inside. Consequently, erosion (through corrasion and hydraulic action) leads to undercutting of the river banks on the outside of the bend. Here slopes may be steep giving **river cliffs**. On the inside there is deposition of silt and the gradient here is gentle. This is called a **slip off slope**.

C Further downstream the river's energy becomes less and erosion is more than balanced by deposition. Here the flood plain is wide. Meanders may be less sinuous having been cut through by the river in times of flood. This will have created **oxbow lakes** (see Question 1). River banks may be quite high (**levees**). When entering the sea or a lake the river water's velocity is checked and its load is deposited. This may create a **delta**. If the level of the sea has risen in the recent past an **estuary** will be formed.

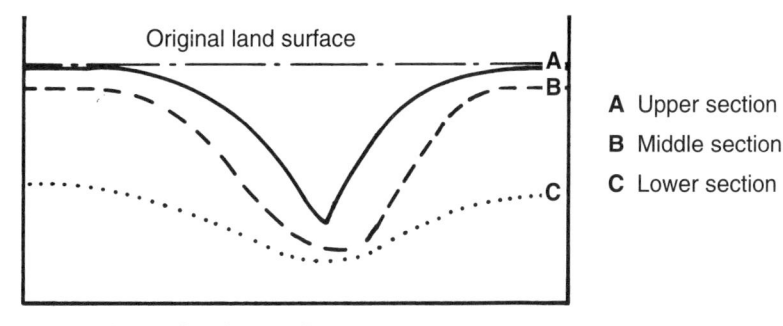

A Upper section
B Middle section
C Lower section

Three typical cross-sections of a river valley

Humans use rivers for a variety of purposes:
- for the transport of goods, e.g. barges on the river Rhine;
- as clearly marked boundary lines, e.g. ten states of the USA use the Mississippi;
- as sources of drinking and irrigation water and of hydroelectric power. For these uses the river has to be dammed and a reservoir created. A narrow damming point, impermeable rock, a large water storage area, a regular supply of water and a sparse population to minimize the risk of pollution are all desirable.

REVISION SUMMARY

If you need to revise this subject more thoroughly, see the relevant topics in the Letts GCSE Geography Study Guide.

The water cycle and rivers and their valleys

QUESTIONS

1 (a) Study Fig. 1 below, which gives information about the hydrological (water) cycle.

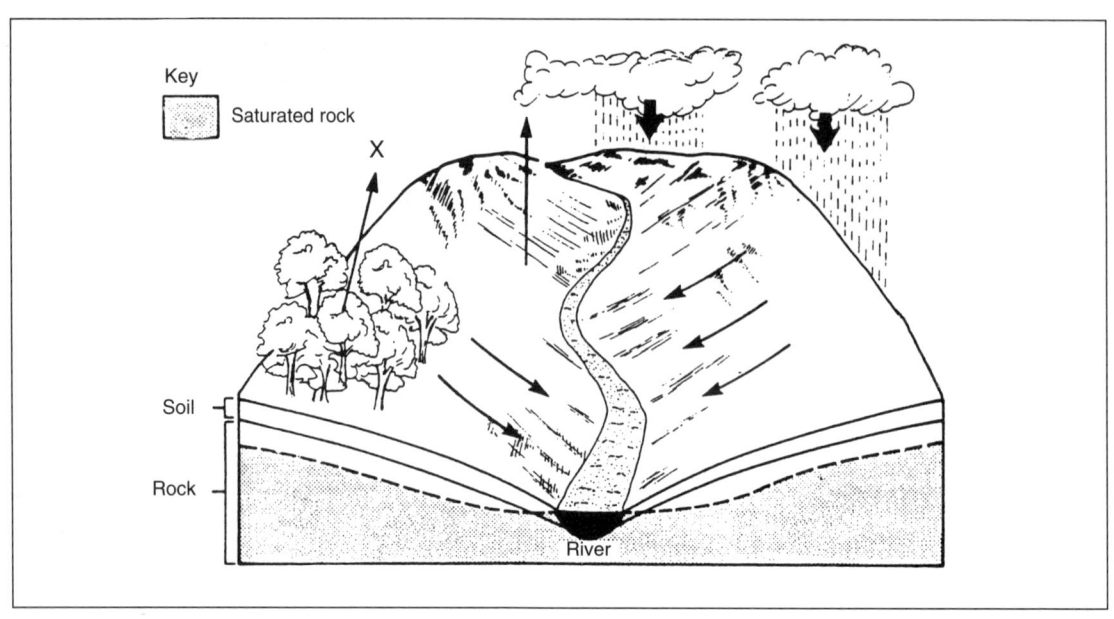

Fig.1

(i) Listed below are some of the processes in the hydrological cycle.

Evaporation   Runoff   Precipitation   Condensation

Show these processes in the correct order on the diagram below. The first process, evaporation, has been done for you. (1)

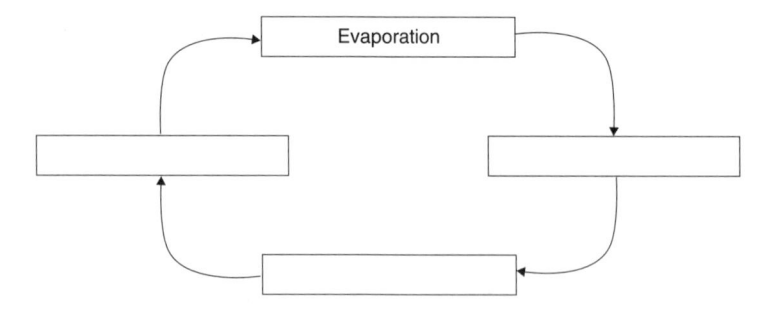

(ii) Name the process which is taking place at X on Fig.1. (1)

(iii) Why will the process you have named in (a) (ii) be greater in summer than in winter? (1)

(iv) What is the name given to the upper level of saturation of soil and rock shown by the pecked line (— — — —) on Fig.1? (1)

(b) Study the OS map extract of Keswick on page 50, scale 1:50 000, showing part of the Lake District in north-west England.

(i) Name the river feature found at map reference 256235. (1)

(ii) Describe the main features of the River Derwent between its exit from Derwent Water (255232) and the western edge of the map extract (240263). (3)

The water cycle and rivers and their valleys

(iii) **Using map evidence only**, name and describe the physical feature formed by the River Derwent at the southern end of Derwent Water. The feature is found to the east of Great Bay. (3)

(iv) Explain how the feature you have described in (b) (iii) may have been formed by the work of the river. (3)

(c) River valleys, such as the one shown on the OS map extract, often suffer from flooding.

(i) Give **two** reasons why flooding takes place in river valleys. (2)

(ii) How may people change the shape of the channel and banks of a river to prevent flooding in the future? (2)

(d) Study Fig. 2, below, which shows part of a river valley.

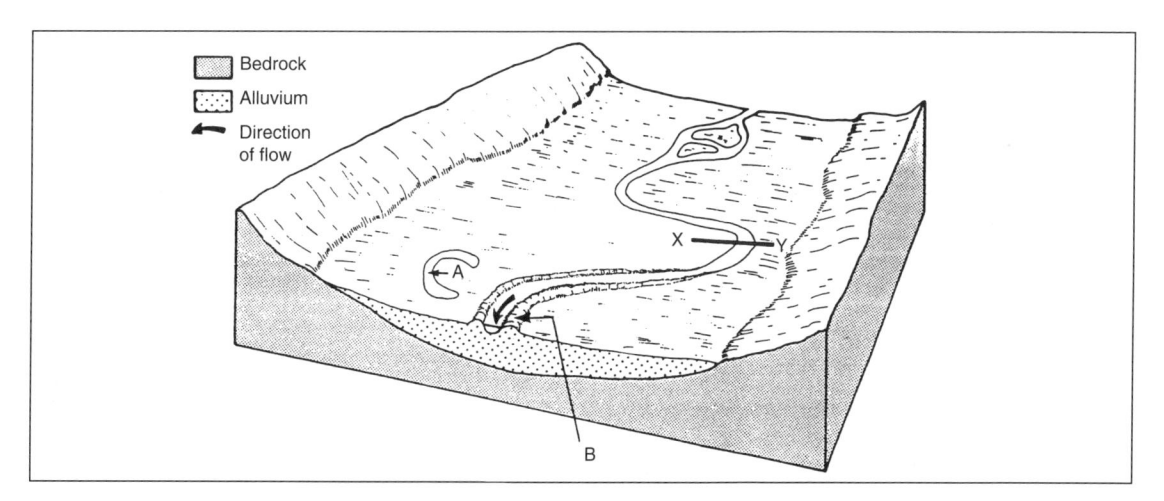

Fig. 2

(i) Name **one** of the physical features labelled A or B. (1)

(ii) Draw a cross-section along the line X–Y to show the shape of the river's channel. Use the grid provided below. On your section, mark with the letter M the position of the river's maximum speed. (2)

Fig. 2b

(iii) Choose **either** feature A or feature B. Explain how the feature you have chosen may have been formed by the river processes. (4)

MEG 1993

2 Coasts

REVISION SUMMARY

Probably the most important agents shaping the coastline are waves, which operate between high and low tide levels. They get their energy from the wind. The stronger the wind and the greater the distance it blows over the sea (its fetch), the higher the wave. Waves are surges of energy through the water. The water itself does not move forward until the wave reaches the coast and begins to break. Waves reaching the coast are often classified as **destructive** or **constructive**. Destructive waves plunge suddenly. Much of their water flows back down the beach (**backwash**) taking material with it, i.e. they erode. They are quite frequent (10–14 per minute). Constructive waves are linked with more gently shelving shores. Their water tends to move up the beach (**swash**) taking material with it, i.e. they build up beaches. They are less frequent (6–8 per minute).

Destructive waves erode the coast by:

- **hydraulic action** – two subdivisions exist: **wave pounding** waves may pound the rock at 30 tonnes per square metre and **hydraulic pressure**, where air in cracks in the rock is alternately compressed and expanded, weakens the rock.
- **corrasion (abrasion)** – cliffs are worn away by pebbles etc. being hurled at them by waves.
- **solution** – certain rocks, e.g. limestone, are soluble in sea water.
- At the same time material carried by the sea is being worn by **attrition**.

The rate of erosion and the nature of the landforms created also depends on the nature and the structure of the rocks making up the coastline. Resistant rocks (e.g. granite and hard sandstones) stand out as headlands. Less resistant rocks (e.g. clays and shales) are eroded more quickly to form bays. Hence, where a coastline consists of alternating bands of hard and soft rocks, a headland and bay coastline will result. Rocks which have been faulted or contain many joints are also susceptible to erosion.

Erosion landforms include **cliffs** and **wave cut platforms, caves, arches, stacks** and **bays**, though the latter may later become areas of deposition. Destructive waves attacking the land create a notch which over time enlarges to create a steep slope called a cliff. The cliff is then undercut by the waves, through the processes of erosion outlined above. The resultant overhang collapses and the cliff face retreats. As it retreats, the wave cut platform at its base widens. Eventually it becomes so wide that the waves lose their energy before reaching the cliff base. The cliff then becomes less steep as it is attacked by subaerial agents.

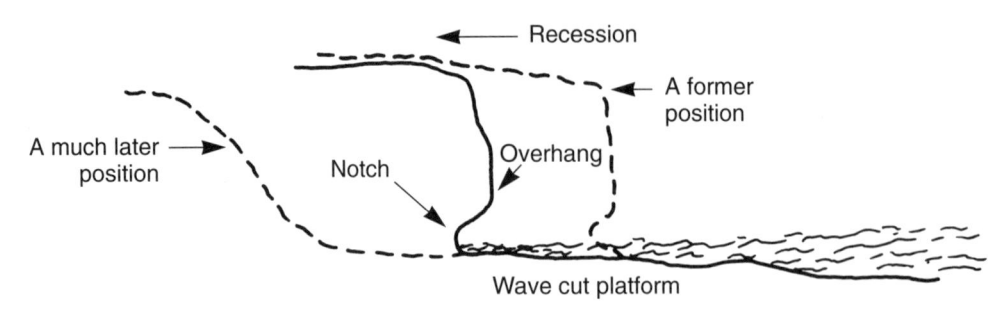

Wave cut platform formation

Cliffs that are made up of rocks that dip seawards tend to be eroded more quickly than those whose rocks dip landwards. If cliffs on a headland are faulted, it is likely that a cave will form at the fault. This may penetrate right through the headland to create an arch. This will eventually collapse to create a stack, then a stump.

Eroded material is moved along a coast by **longshore drift** and creates features of deposition elsewhere – usually where the coastline has a gentle gradient and the waves are constructive. The material moved may be added to by material washed down by rivers. Longshore drift occurs because most waves approach the shore obliquely and, therefore, carry material along in a zigzag fashion, as shown in the diagram on page 9.

Coasts

REVISION SUMMARY

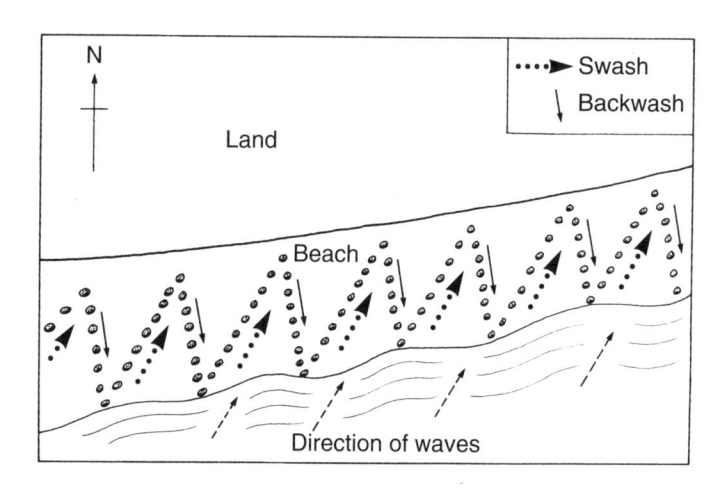

Landforms created by the deposition of material include: **beaches, spits, mud flats** and **deltas**. A beach is a stretch of sand/shingle/pebbles deposited between HWM and LWM along a coast. It is a consequence of constructive waves and longshore drift. Beaches occur where the input of material exceeds depletion. Bay head beaches are usually much smaller and result from waves losing energy within a bay.

If a beach coastline changes direction, the deposited material may carry on being deposited in a straight line out to sea. This narrow finger of sand/shingle is called a spit and may become several kilometres long. Sand may pile up, through the action of the wind, into dunes. They may become fixed by marram grass. Eventually, the end of the spit may swing around to form a 'hook'. Behind the spit in the almost calm waters, mud and silt will settle and create a salt marsh.

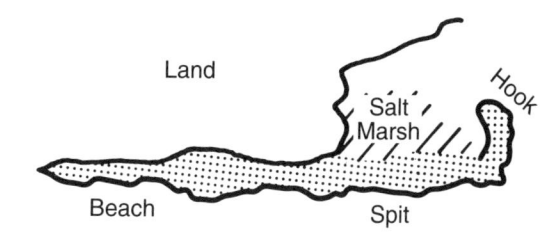

Deltas can occur where rivers enter the sea (or a lake). The river's velocity is abruptly checked, so it loses its energy and drops its load. Reaction to sea water helps deposition, as clay particles will cohere more readily. Deposition is also helped if the sea has low or no tides. Hence, deltas are common at the mouths of rivers entering the Mediterranean sea, e.g. Nile, Rhône. Deltas provide areas of flat, often fertile, land.

If sea level has risen over recent geological time, relative to the land, the coastline will become irregular with inlets at the mouths of rivers. These are **estuaries**. If the 'drowning' by the sea is greater the whole lower course of a number of river valleys may be flooded permanently creating a **ria**.

Coastal areas are increasingly affected by human activities. In an attempt to preserve their beaches some resorts build artificial barriers (groynes) at right angles to the shore to prevent the longshore drift of sand. This may cause beaches further along the coast to disappear as their sand supply diminishes and also any cliffs there to suffer greater erosion. Removal of sand supply and shingle from the sea bed some distance out for the building industry is also thought to be depleting beaches and thereby increasing erosion. Industrial and tourist developments on estuaries and small bays may destroy the breeding grounds of migrating birds. Wildlife and sometimes human life also suffers because of pollution. Sewage is a major pollution problem along the coasts of many developed countries. Not only does it contaminate beaches, it also takes oxygen from the sea, harming marine life. Pollution from farmland fertilisers, polluted water from estuarine industries and oil from ships washing out their tanks are other pollutants which mar coastal environments.

If you need to revise this subject more thoroughly, see the relevant topics in the *Letts* GCSE *Geography Study Guide*.

2 Coasts

QUESTIONS

1   Study Fig. 1, a sketch map of the Pegwell Bay area in East Kent, and the aerial photograph below which shows part of the same area.

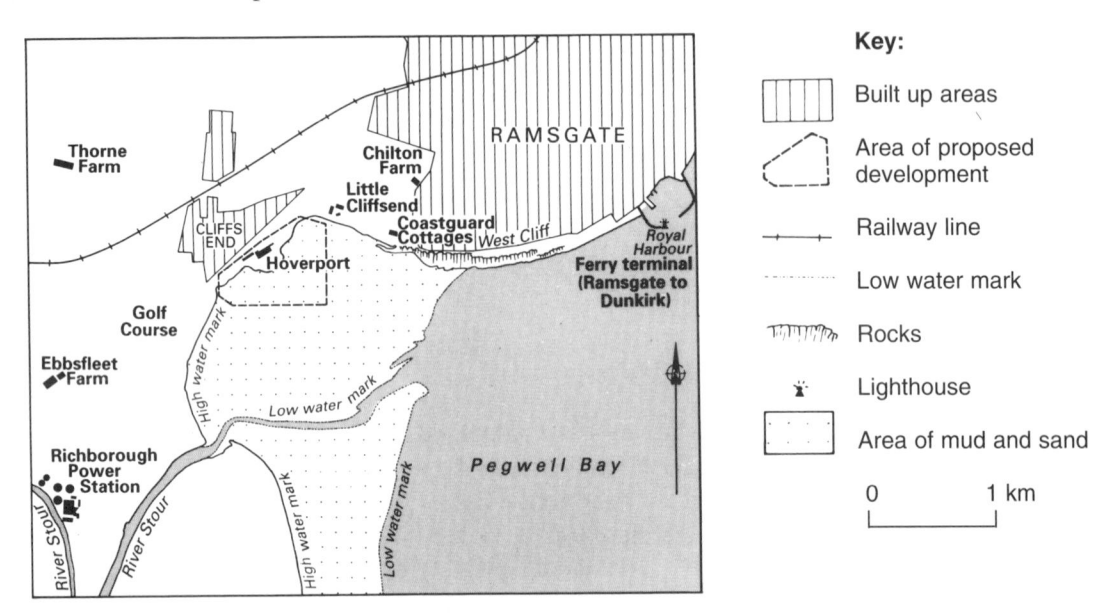

Fig. 1 Pegwell Bay

Key:
- Built up areas
- Area of proposed development
- Railway line
- Low water mark
- Rocks
- Lighthouse
- Area of mud and sand

0   1 km

A part of Pegwell Bay

By courtesy of Aerofilms

Coasts

(a) (i) Name the features X and Y on the photograph.

   (ii) Using evidence from the map and the photograph state **four** other uses that are made of this coastal area.

   (iii) State **one** piece of evidence which suggests that the photograph was taken at high tide. (7)

(b) Study Fig. 1 and Fig. 2, which provides details of major development proposals for the area identified on the map and the photograph.

	DEVELOPMENT PROPOSALS FOR PEGWELL BAY	
Overall aim	– To create a unique coastal environment.	
Means	– By creating a shallow recreational basin protected by a ring of artificial islands. These islands would create a new wildlife sanctuary while the existing beach area will be retained. The site is planned as an all weather recreation/leisure and small conference complex, a waterside residential community and dinghy marina with supporting retail outlets. The residential units will be developed for the personal and business tourist markets, second and permanent home buyers. The recreational/leisure facilities will be available to the residents and to the general public on a membership basis.	
Site details	– Residential units Retail units Recreation/leisure Artificial basin Artificial islands Dinghy berths	– Approx 400 – Approx 5,000 sq. ft. – 7.5 acres – Approx 70 acres – Approx 3 acres+ – 100+

Fig. 2

   (i) Give **two** facts which show that the developers are concerned about the natural environment of the area.

   (ii) What will need to be demolished before the development can take place?

   (iii) Suggest why it is necessary to construct the artificial islands.

   (iv) Suggest **two** reasons why it is proposed to create a shallow recreational basin when a large bay already exists. (6)

(c) The residents of Cliffsend have divided opinions about the scheme.

   (i) Suggest **three** reasons why many are likely to support the scheme.

   (ii) Suggest **one** possible objection they might have. (4)

(d) Pollution is an increasing problem along coastlines. For an area you have studied where this problem is or has been particularly serious:

   (i) Name the area and describe the type(s) of pollution involved.

   (ii) Explain what measures are being taken or were needed to reduce the level of pollution. (8)

ULEAC 1993

3 Weathering and glaciation

REVISION SUMMARY

Weathering is the break-up of rock *in situ* on the surface of the land through the action of atmospheric and biological agents. It is the first stage in soil formation and is an essential preliminary to erosion by rivers, ice, the sea and wind. There are three main types of weathering.

Physical (or mechanical) weathering: this breaks up the rock into smaller and smaller pieces, but there is no chemical change. It is caused by: (i) large temperature changes within a rock and/or (ii) by the alternate freezing and thawing of water, both causing stresses within the rocks so that they fracture. Process (ii) is often called frost shattering. The products of such weathering are angular in shape and may under gravity slip down slopes, collecting at the bottom as a scree slope. Physical weathering is common in the cooler and drier parts of the world.

Chemical weathering: this causes the rotting of rocks, which are decomposed by carbon dioxide and other organic acids. Such weathering is more common in the warmer and wetter parts of the world. Soluble rocks are more prone to this type of weathering. Much of the weathered material is subsequently removed in solution. The role of chemical weathering has become more significant during this century as human beings have released more chemicals into the atmosphere. Some of these return to the ground as acid rain, speeding up chemical weathering.

Biological weathering: this describes those processes where plant roots prise open rocks (physical) and humic acids from vegetation and bacteria attack the rocks (chemical).

It is important to realise that all three types of weathering usually act together.

GLACIATION

There have been Ice Ages, i.e. periods when ice covered significant portions of the Earth's surface, regularly during the Earth's history. Just 18 000 years ago much of the British Isles was covered by ice. During these cold phases, snow which fell in winter gradually lasted longer and longer on the ground until it became permanent. Snow which fell in hollows gradually became deeper until the lower layers of snow turned to ice through compression. Ice collected high up in valleys and then moved down them as glaciers. Sometimes these glaciers, reaching lowland areas, merged to form ice sheets.

Ice moving downhill is able to erode, using materials made available to it by earlier weathering and river action. The material it carries is called moraine (see diagram for further details).

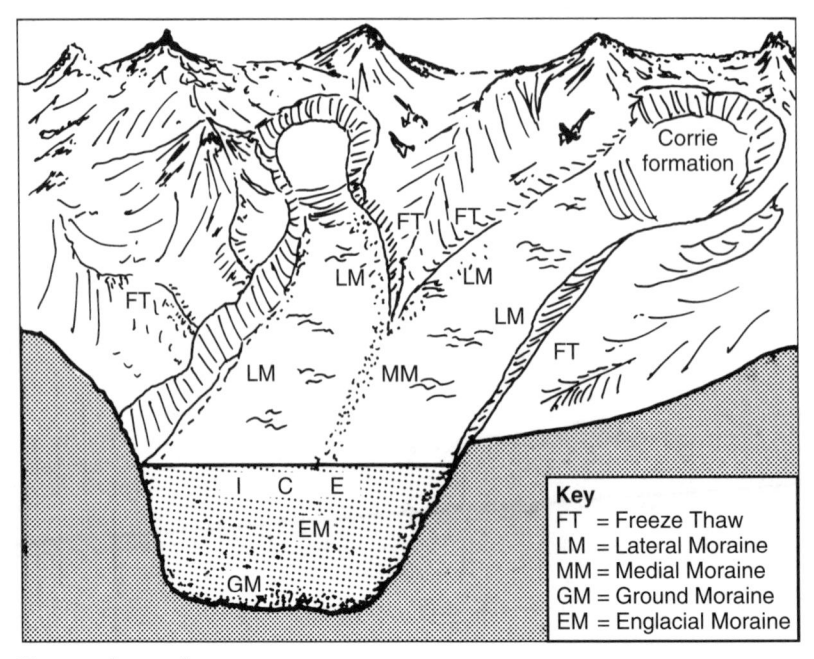

Key
FT = Freeze Thaw
LM = Lateral Moraine
MM = Medial Moraine
GM = Ground Moraine
EM = Englacial Moraine

Types of moraine

Weathering and glaciation 3

REVISION SUMMARY

The two main processes of ice erosion are **abrasion** and **plucking**. Abrasion is the grinding away and polishing of rock on the valley floor and sides by the moraine (load) sticking out of the moving glacier. Near the base and sides of the glacier ice melts into and refreezes around jointed or protruding rock and, as the glacier then moves, it pulls these rocks away. This is plucking. Above the glacier, **freeze thaw** will be active giving the supraglacial landscape a jagged appearance and providing the glacier with a constant supply of material.

Features of glacial erosion include glacial valleys or troughs and above them **corries** (or cirques), **arêtes, pyramidal peaks** and **hanging valleys. Glaciated valleys** were once river valleys. These were deepened and widened by the processes mentioned above to become **U-shaped troughs**. Corries were hillside hollows which were enlarged and deepened by ice. They consequently became lake-filled. Arêtes are the narrow ridges between the back walls of corries, while a pyramidal peak marks the junction of four corries.

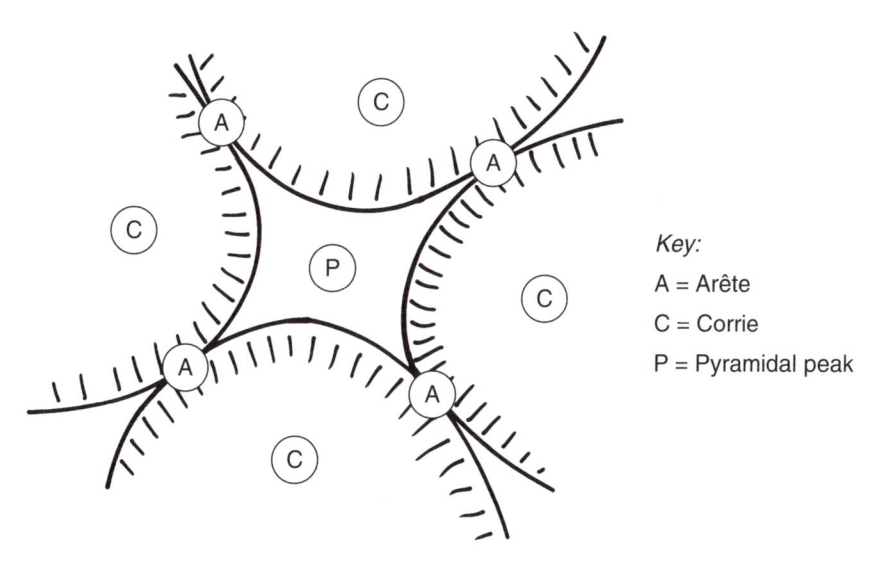

Key:
A = Arête
C = Corrie
P = Pyramidal peak

Hanging valleys are tributary valleys, with floors which are now found well above the main valley. They were deepened much less by the smaller, tributary glaciers occupying them, than was the main valley by its larger glacier. The drops between the two valley floors are now frequently marked by waterfalls.

Where valley glaciers or ice sheets move into lowlands, the moraine they carry will be deposited as they melt (ground moraine or boulder clay). If deposition takes place at the front of a stationary ice sheet of glacier (from melting streams) sometimes a long, ridge-like **terminal moraine** may form. Such moraines at the end of a valley glacier may in effect deepen a glacially eroded hollow and create or enlarge a ribbon lake.

If you need to revise this subject more thoroughly, see the relevant topics in the *Letts* GCSE *Geography Study Guide.*

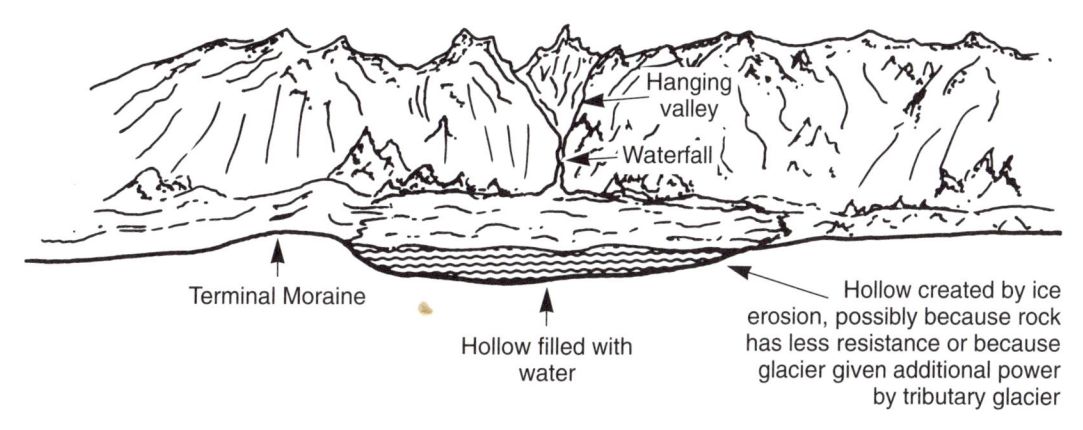

Terminal Moraine — Hollow filled with water — Hanging valley — Waterfall — Hollow created by ice erosion, possibly because rock has less resistance or because glacier given additional power by tributary glacier

Ribbon lake formation

3 Weathering and glaciation

QUESTIONS

1 (a) Study the photograph below and the OS map extract (found on page 51) which show a glaciated area in the Lake District.

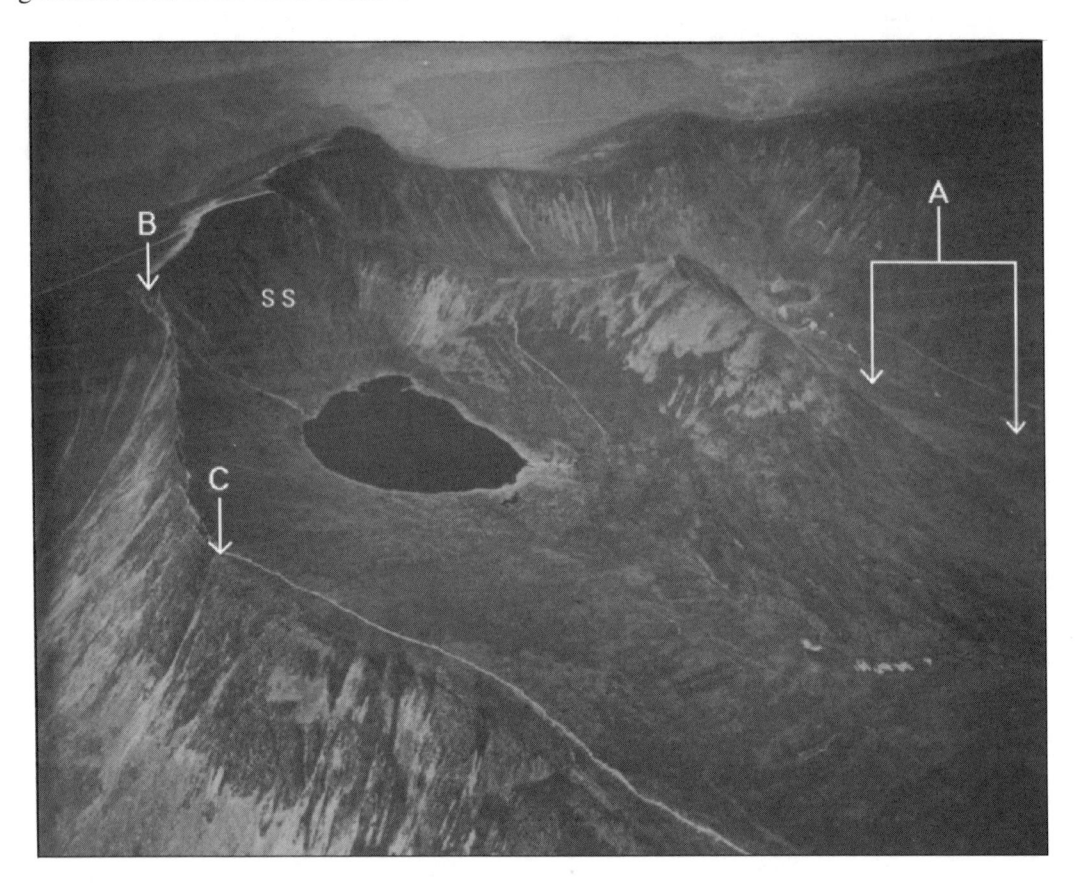

(i) Name the landforms lettered A, B and C from the following list:

Striding Edge   Glenridding   Helvellyn   (3)

(ii) Which of these is an arête?   (1)

(iii) Name the lake in the background of the photograph.   (1)

(b) The steep slope marked **SS** on the photograph is an end product of weathering and erosion. On page 15 is a sketch of such a slope showing some weathering processes taking place.

(i) Name the three types of weathering shown by the lettered arrows.   (3)

(ii) Which of these was most important during glacial times?   (1)

(iii) 1. What typical feature would you see on a landscape experiencing this type of weathering?

2. Add this feature to the diagram.   (2)

Weathering and glaciation 3

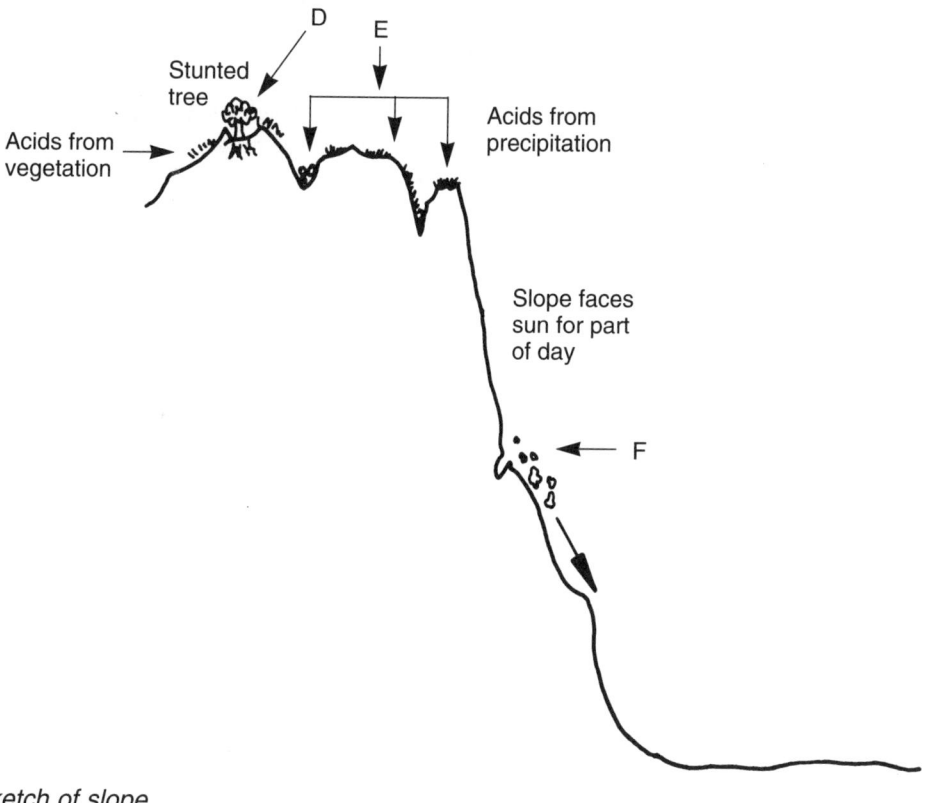

QUESTIONS

Sketch of slope

(Labels on sketch: Stunted tree, D, E, Acids from vegetation, Acids from precipitation, Slope faces sun for part of day, F)

(c) The whole of the area in the south-eastern half of grid square 3415, surrounding Red Tarn, is called a corrie.

   (i) Using OS map and photographic evidence, describe its characteristic features. (3)

   (ii) Using labelled diagrams, explain how it was formed. (6)

(d) Some of the footpaths of this area stand out clearly as white lines on the photograph because of erosion.

   (i) Explain fully, giving at least three reasons, why footpath erosion begun by hill walkers, then worsened by a range of geomorphic processes, is often severe in regions like this. (6)

   (ii) What can be done to try and reduce the rate of soil erosion on such slopes? (4)

(In the style of WJEC)

4 Weather and climate

REVISION SUMMARY

Weather relates to everyday changes in the atmosphere over an area; the climate is the averaging out of weather over a number of years.

Rainfall, high or low **temperature, fog, wind** and **sunshine amounts** are called **weather elements**. Factors which affect these elements and make them what they are, are termed **weather** or **climatic factors**. These include **latitude, altitude, seasons**, whether one is close to or far from the sea (**continentality**) and **ocean currents**.

- **Latitude** is important because the higher the latitude, the lower the angle of the Sun in the sky. The lower the angle, the less warmth the Sun gives.
- **Seasons** – In addition, because of the tilt of the Earth in relation to the Sun, higher latitudes have much more variation in the height of the Sun in the sky during the year and much more variation in the length of day and night than places in the tropics. So in northern Scandinavia (65 °N) days are long and the Sun fairly high in the sky during summer making it tolerably warm. In winter, the Sun is low in the sky, the days are very short (2 or 3 hours) and it is very cold. Near the Equator, the length of night and day and the height of the Sun vary little, so the weather and climate is similar throughout the year.
- **Continentality** – The sea, e.g. the North Atlantic, takes longer to warm up and cool down than the land surface, e.g. Europe, so it acts as a reservoir of heat in winter and coolness in summer. If winds blow from the Atlantic on to western Europe, i.e. are **onshore**, then this warmth or coolness is brought on to the land.

These controls and others are shown more clearly on the diagram below.

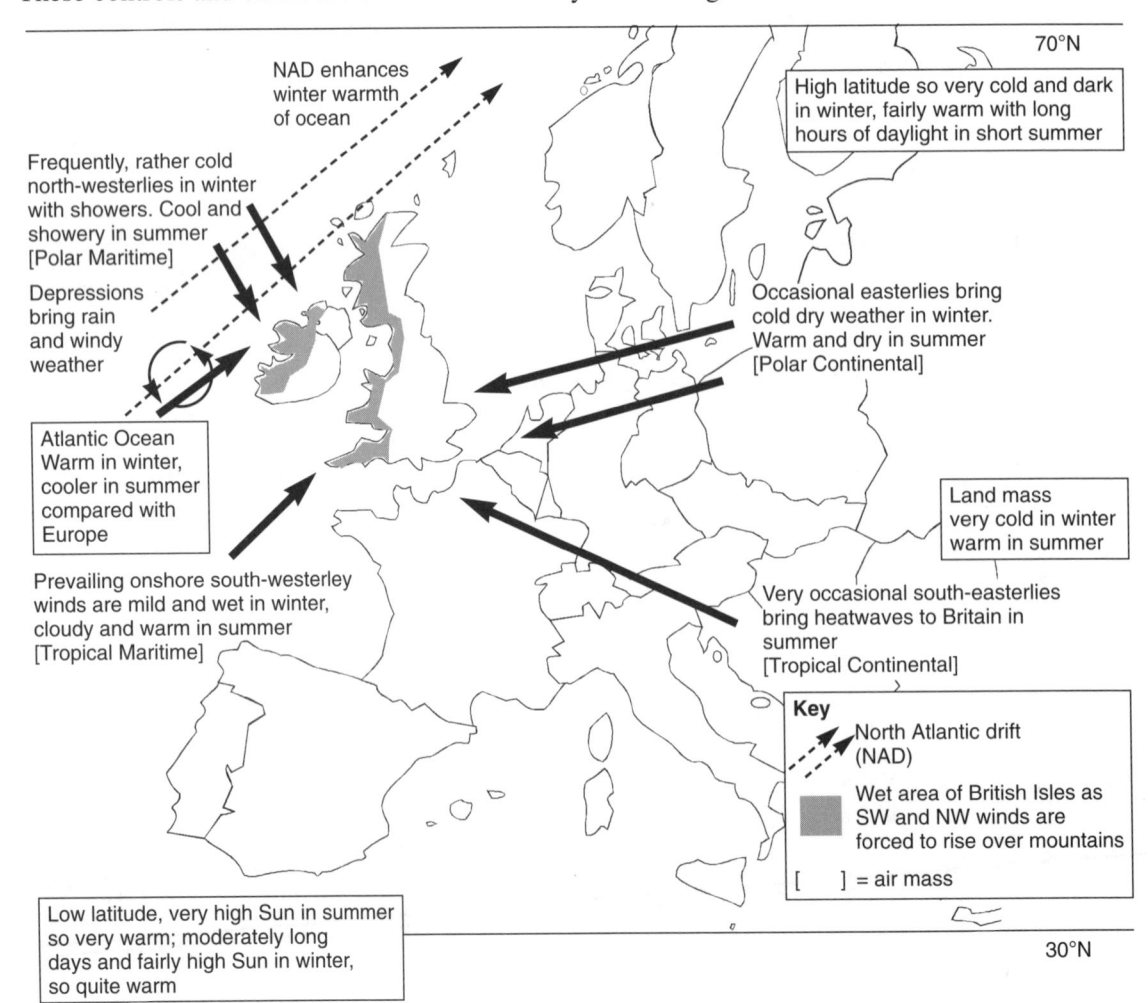

Factors affecting weather and climate of British Isles and adjacent parts of Europe

Weather and climate 4

Rainfall, or more correctly precipitation as this includes snow and hail, is the result of air rising, cooling, condensation taking place to form clouds, with precipitation often ensuing. Rainfall is usually classified into three types: **convectional, relief** (orographic) and **frontal** (cyclonic). This classification is based on the cause of the air rising. Convectional rain results from air rising because of the Sun heating the ground and warming the air above; relief rain results from air being forced to rise over high ground; frontal rain results from warmer air being forced to rise by colder air in a frontal depression.

REVISION SUMMARY

CHARACTERISTICS OF DEPRESSIONS AND ANTICYCLONES

Air pressure is measured on a barometer and is usually expressed in millibars (mb). In our latitudes, low pressure is termed a **depression**, high pressure is called an **anticyclone**.

Depression

Air moves anticlockwise, converges and rises.

Conflict of air masses causes further rising of air and precipitation at cold, warm and occluded fronts.

Weather: cloudy, windy, rain or showers. Mild in winter. Cool in summer.

Air quality good, as pollutants are dispersed.

Anticyclone

Air moves clockwise, diverges and subsides.

Homogeneous air mass and air stable. No fronts.

Weather: little cloud, light winds, dry, night fogs. Cold in winter (frosts), warm in summer.

Air quality often poor. If a temperature inversion exists pollutants are trapped near the ground, giving smog in winter.
Ozone in summer in cities caused by bright sunshine on car fumes.

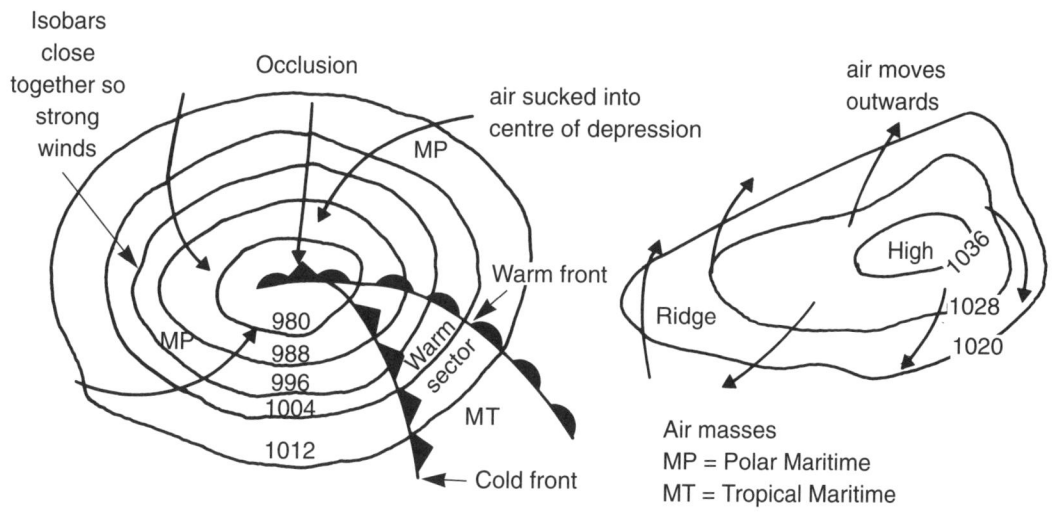

Isobars close together so strong winds

Occlusion

air sucked into centre of depression

MP

Warm front

980
988
996
1004
1012

MP

Warm sector

MT

Cold front

air moves outwards

High 1036
Ridge 1028
1020

Air masses
MP = Polar Maritime
MT = Tropical Maritime

Weather elements, when combined together and averaged out over a period of 20–30 years, constitute the climate of a place. No two places have precisely the same climate, but places with similar climates can be grouped together. All places within a particular climatic region normally also share similar natural vegetation and soils. This is because these three components of the environment are interrelated.

Letts
Q&A

17

4 Weather and climate

REVISION SUMMARY

SUMMARIES OF INTERRELATIONSHIPS IN THREE CLIMATIC REGIONS

Name and location	Equatorial: Amazon Basin, Congo Basin, Indonesia	Monsoon: South-east Asia	Cool Temperate Continental: Prairies and Steppes
Climate	Hot (27 °C) and wet (1500–2000 mm) all year round.	Tropical Monsoon. Hot/wet and cooler/dry season. Sometimes very wet (1000–2000 mm).	Long, cold winters with a little snow. Warm, showery summers.
Vegetation	Rainforests. Great variety of hardwoods. Forest appears green all year.	Monsoon forests. Jungle, almost impenetrable on hills, cleared on lowlands.	Short grassland of steppe and prairie types.
Soils	Red, deep, rather infertile – latosols.	On hills, tropical soils ravaged by erosion. In valleys, alluvial soils.	Fertile black earths (chernozems) or browner prairie soils.
Native way of life	Shifting subsistence agriculture. Crops – manioc, yams, hunting and fishing.	Intensive subsistence rice farming in valleys. Double cropping of rice. In cooler areas, rice and wheat. Terraced hillside prevents soil loss.	Nomadic herding or hunting, e.g. Red Indians and bison.
Recent modifications	Forests felled for timber, mining and farming. Plantations set up.	Green revolution – hybrid strains. Intermediate technology, tea plantations.	Extensive grain farming – wheat, barley, some maize.

If you need to revise this subject more thoroughly, see the relevant topics in the Letts GCSE Geography Study Guide.

The British Isles experience a Cool Temperate Western Margin type climate. Winters are mild and wet, summers are not too warm and still fairly wet. The region has a natural vegetation of deciduous forest – most of it cleared for farming – and possesses quite deep, fairly fertile brown forest soils.

Weather and climate 4

1 (a) Study the information about the Equatorial Rain Forests on Fig. 1.

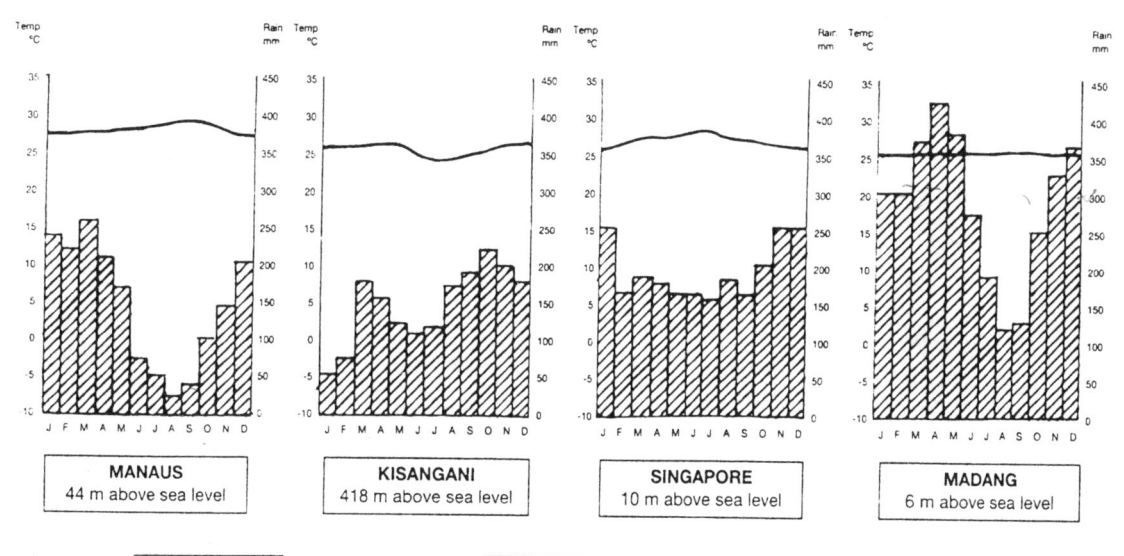

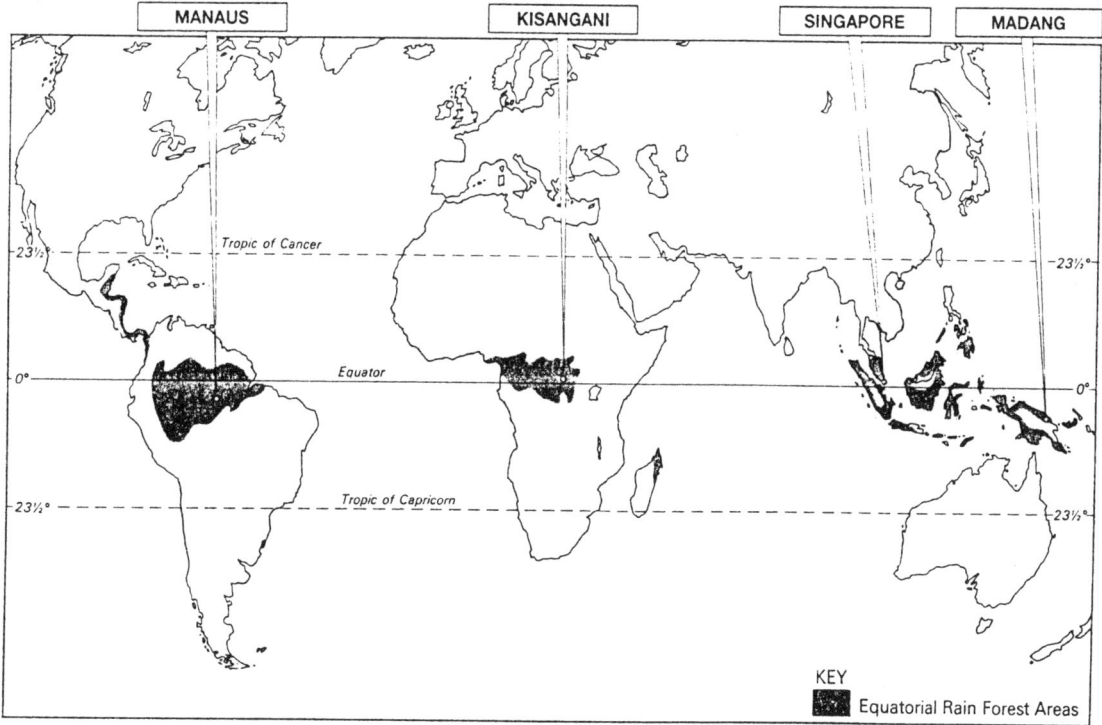

Fig. 1

(i) Describe the distribution of the Equatorial Rain Forest areas. (3)

(ii) What is the average rainfall in Madang in January? (1)

(iii) Why do Equatorial Rain Forests have a high annual rainfall? (3)

(iv) What is the meaning of the term 'annual range of temperature'? (2)

(v) State briefly why the annual range of temperature in Equatorial Rain Forest areas is so small. (2)

4 Weather and climate

QUESTIONS

(b) Study the weather map, Fig. 2.

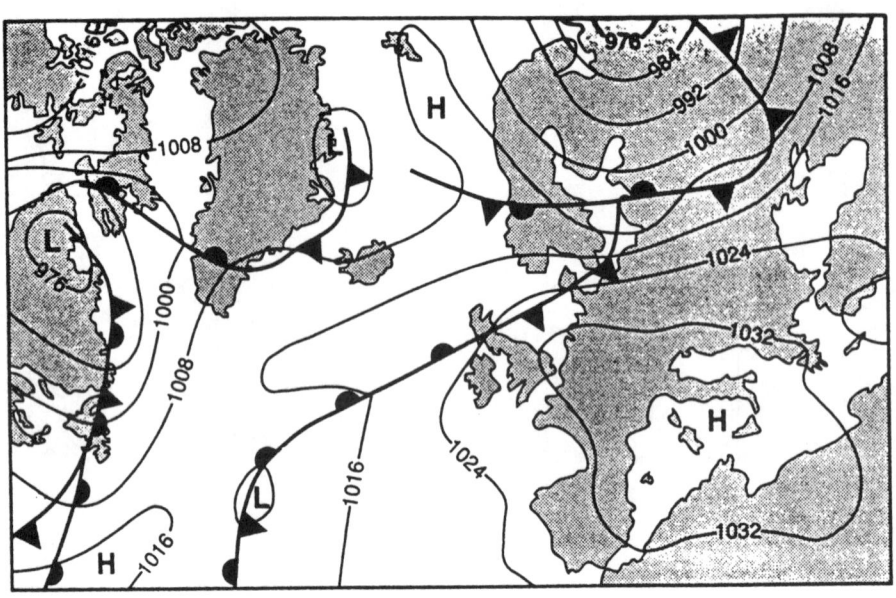

Fig. 2   © The Guardian 14.12.91

(i) What units are used to measure atmospheric pressure? (1)

(ii) What type of pressure system is shown over most of western Europe? (1)

(iii) Winds over southern England on 14 December were light and southerly.

(A) How does Fig. 2 suggest that the winds were light? (1)

(B) Explain why the winds were southerly. (3)

(c) Study Fig. 3, a report on the very poor air quality conditions which existed in much of England at the time of the weather map shown in Fig. 2.

Phew! What a wheezer

Motorists in London were urged to stop driving by the Government yesterday as air pollution reached the highest levels since records began in 1976.

It was the first time the Department of Environment has called for voluntary restraint in using cars, which are the main cause of the 'very poor' air quality recorded at every one of the department's monitoring stations in the capital.

Asthmatics and people with chest complaints were urged by the Department of Health to stay indoors as much as possible and to seek medical advice if they begin to suffer from coughing, wheezing or shortness of breath.

Joggers and others taking exercise outdoors were advised to stop until the current cold, still weather ends.

People should avoid using streets with heavy traffic but that did not mean it was unsafe to go to work, or necessary to wear a mask.

A spokeswoman for the department appealed to the public to use public transport whenever possible.

There are four categories of air quality: very good, good, poor and very poor. Very poor is recorded when nitrogen dioxide reaches 300 parts per billion. Yesterday 382 parts per billion were recorded in central London, 388 in west London and 423 in south-west London.

In some parts of Europe, such as Holland and Denmark, local authorities can stop traffic and restrict industrial emission if air quality standards drop as far as those in London.

Fig. 3

Weather and climate 4

QUESTIONS

(i) Use Fig. 3 to name:

(A) the gas used as a measure of air quality. (1)

(B) one health problem caused by the very poor air quality. (1)

(ii) Suggest how the weather conditions shown in Fig. 2 would help cause the air quality found over much of the United Kingdom. (2)

(iii) Why should governments encourage motorists not to use their cars in such weather conditions? (4)

SEG 1993

2 (a) Study Fig. 4, the satellite image and Figs. 5 and 6, synoptic charts.

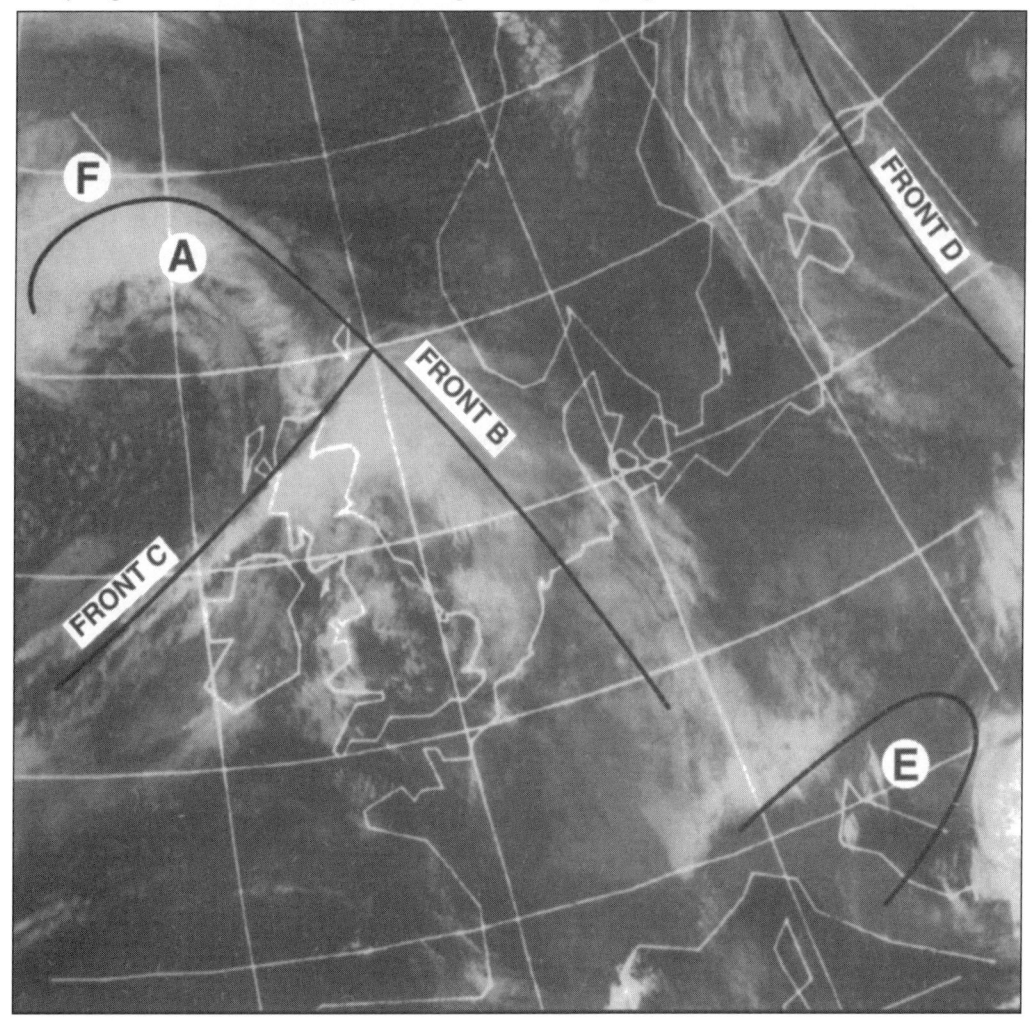

(Reproduced with kind permission from Dundee University)

Fig. 4 Satellite image – 3 a.m. 19 December 1991

4 Weather and climate

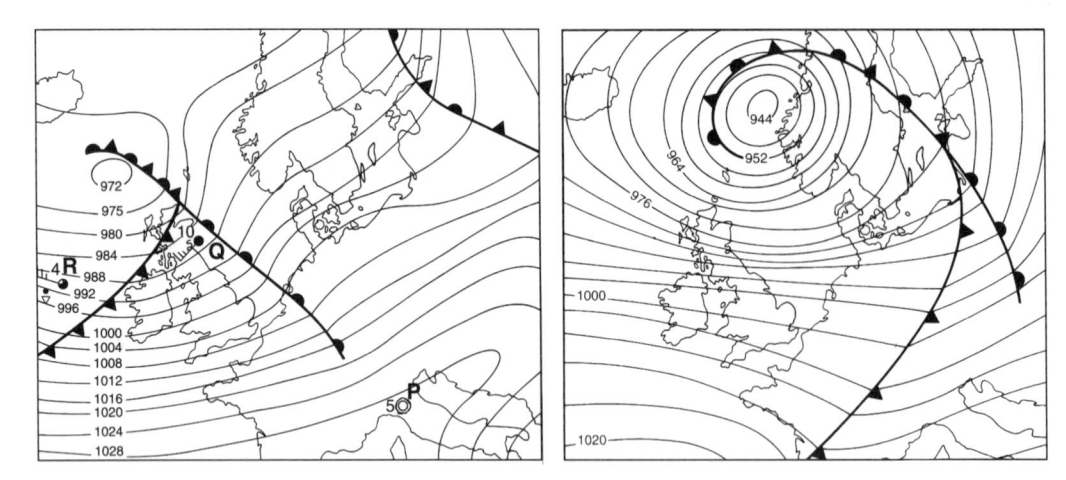

QUESTIONS

Fig. 5 Weather map – 3 a.m.
19 December 1991

Fig. 6 Weather map – 3 a.m.
20 December 1991

The satellite image has several features labelled. Using Fig. 5 to help you, identify

(i) weather system A, B, C, D, pressure feature E. (5)

(ii) Suggest **two** pieces of evidence that the line marking front B on Fig. 4 is located more than 100 km farther east than it should be. (2)

(iii) Explain why the cloud belt is curved at F. (2)

Study Fig. 5 only.

(iv) Describe the weather at Weather Station R. (3)

(v) In what way can the **satellite image** help support your description of the weather at Weather Station R? (2)

(b) Using Fig. 5, explain the temperature conditions at Weather Stations P, Q and R.

(i) Weather Station P

(ii) Weather Station Q

(iii) Weather Station R (6)

(c) Refer to Fig. 6, a weather map showing the situation 24 hours later.

(i) Describe how weather system A and its fronts changed over the 24 hours. Give **four** changes. (4)

(ii) Write a weather report to describe and explain **two** features of the weather for Britain at 3 a.m. 20 December 1991 (Fig. 6). (6)

WJEC 1993 (slightly adapted)

Population and resources 5

DISTRIBUTION OF POPULATION

At present there are over 5 billion people living on Earth. The world's population, however, is not spread evenly across the globe. In fact, half the world's people occupy only one twentieth of the land surface. Human beings can only live where conditions are right for life, so people are attracted to the most suitable areas. Few people live where a hostile environment or the lack of essential resources would make life difficult to sustain.

Most people live where conditions are favourable, for example:

- where farmland is fertile and suitable for growing crops
- where the climate is pleasant and equable
- where important minerals such as coal are found
- where flat land allows towns and cities to be built.

Few people live where conditions are unfavourable, for example:

- high latitudes where temperatures are too cold
- hot deserts which are too dry
- jungles which are too dense to penetrate
- mountains which are too steep to build on.

The number of people per unit area is called the **population density**. In some parts of the world the population density is high. For example, parts of Hong Kong have over 6000 people living in every square kilometre. Actual figures for population density can be misleading.

It is not the total number of people that is important but whether or not an area has sufficient resources to support the number of people who want to live there.

If an area cannot support its population then that area is said to be **overpopulated**. For example, the Netherlands has a population density of 970 people per square kilometre but is not overpopulated because it is a wealthy country which has developed its resources to a point where it is able to support its population. Ethiopia has a population density of 45 people per square kilometre but, in parts, is considered overpopulated because a rapidly growing population, a series of droughts and agricultural mismanagement have used up the country's resources of land and food at a rate too great to be sustained.

POPULATION PYRAMIDS

The shapes of **population pyramids** can tell you quite a lot about the countries they represent. A triangular shape, like that shown in Fig. 1 below, will tell you that this country is part of the developing world, where birth rates are high (hence the broad base) and expectation of life is fairly low (hence the rapidly narrowing top). If the pyramid is more pillar shaped, like that shown in Fig. 2 below, it signifies that this country is in the developed world. Here the birth rate is much lower – almost as low as the death rate – so this country's population is virtually static, as long as there is no significant gain or loss from migration.

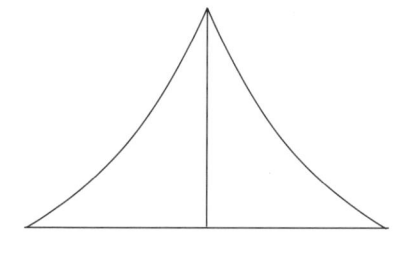

Fig. 1

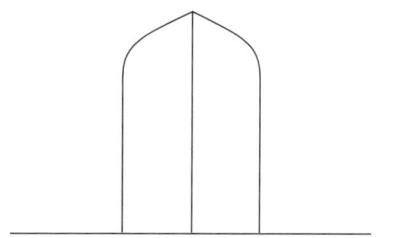

Fig. 2

REVISION SUMMARY

If you need to revise this subject more thoroughly, see the relevant topics in the *Letts GCSE Geography Study Guide*.

5 Population and resources

QUESTIONS

1 (a) Study the age/sex pyramids shown in Fig. 3.

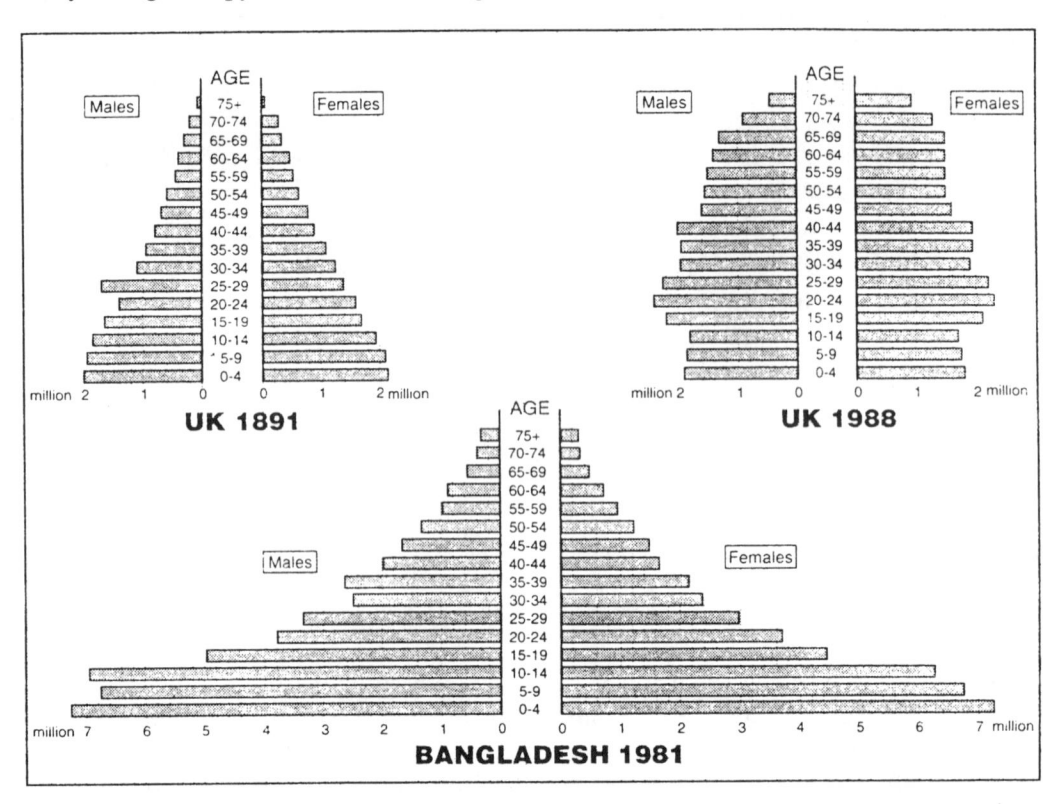

Fig. 3

    (i) What is a census? (1)

    (ii) In what ways is the shape of the pyramid for the UK in 1891 similar to that for Bangladesh in 1981? (2)

    (iii) Describe the changes that have taken place to the United Kingdom's age/sex pyramid between 1891 and 1988. (3)

    (iv) Explain the issues which result from the changes in the UK's population structure. (4)

    (v) Why do some people disagree with controlling population growth? (3)

(b) Study Fig. 4 on page 25, showing the population density of different countries.

    (i) What is the meaning of the term population density? (1)

    (ii) Which of the countries named on Fig. 4 has the highest population density? (1)

    (iii) Why can information on population density be more useful than figures which show only a country's total population? (2)

    (iv) 'Physical factors cause variations in population density throughout the world.' Comment on this statement, with reference to places you have studied. (8)

Population and resources

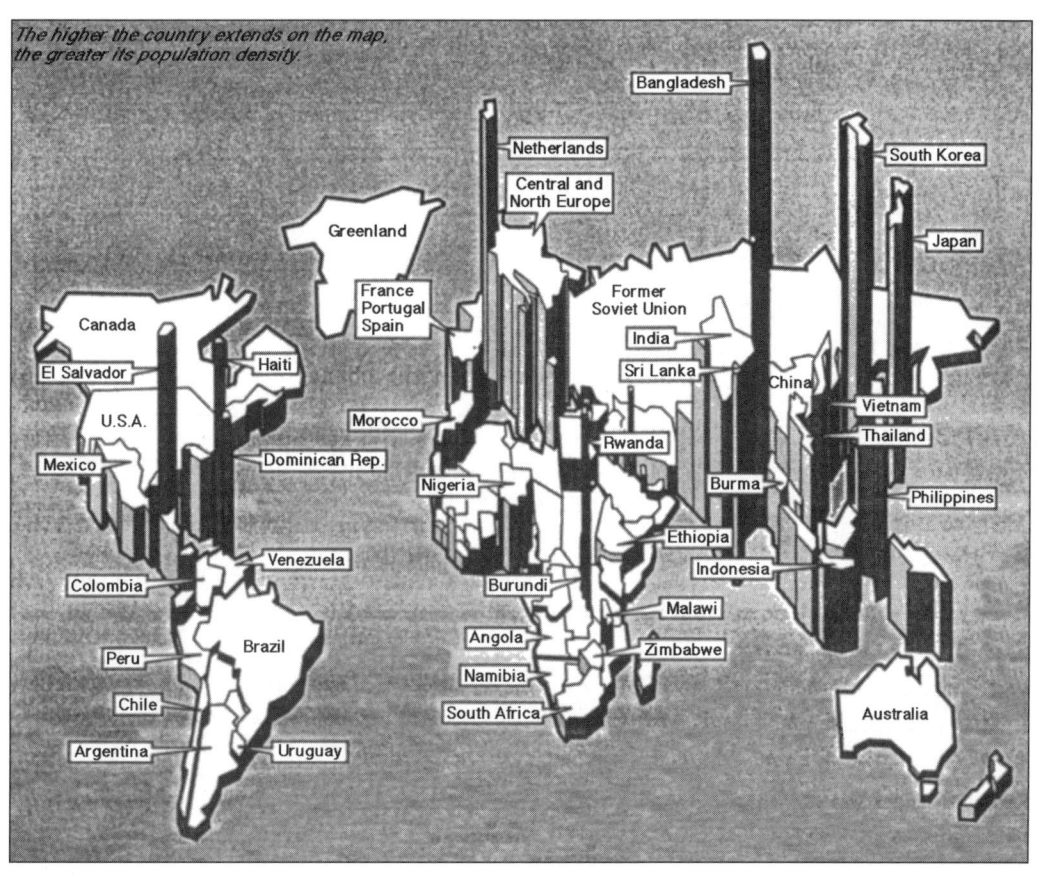

QUESTIONS

Fig. 4

SEG 1993

6 Settlement

REVISION SUMMARY

The **site** of a settlement is the place where that settlement is built. The siting of early settlements depended on one or more of the following factors:

- defensive sites, such as on the top of a hill or in the bend of a river, were chosen to guard against attack
- wet point sites were close to rivers for water supply
- dry point sites avoided flood plains and marshy areas
- bridging points were built at the easiest place to cross a river
- proximity to building materials
- good farm land to produce food
- a supply of fuel for cooking and heating.

The **situation** of a settlement describes its location in relation to other factors. The growth of a settlement depends on its site, its situation and its **function**. The function is the main purpose for that settlement. Small settlements may have only one function while larger settlements may have many functions. For example:

- most **market towns** are old settlements. They began when many of the population were farmers who needed somewhere to sell their produce and to buy the items they needed such as seeds and tools.
- an **administration centre** is usually quite large and deals with all the work involved in the running of an area, such as a county. There are many offices, including the county hall, law courts and police headquarters.
- a **holiday resort** is a place people visit for holidays. The main function of a resort is to provide a place where people can enjoy themselves and relax.
- a **port** is a place where goods are imported into the country and exported to other countries.
- an **industrial centre** is a town where industry dominates. It may be just one type of industry, such as a coal mine, or a variety of factories.
- a **route centre** is built around a place where many roads meet.
- a **residential centre** provides homes for people. All towns are residential centres.

THE LAYOUT OF TOWNS

Urban land use is usually studied using a model. The Concentric Ring Model (after Burgess) and the Sector Model (after Hoyt) are two common models used in geography. Land use in a typical British city is a combination of these two models, as shown below.

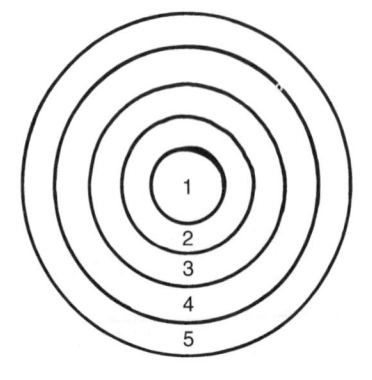

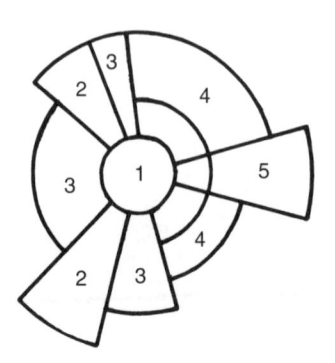

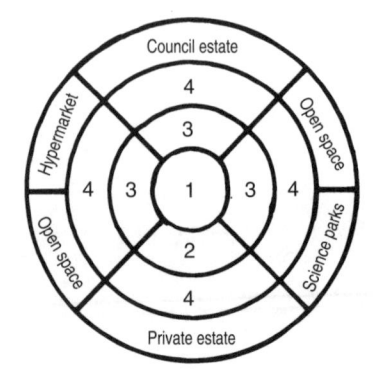

Key: 1 = CBD, 2 = Transitional zone, 3 = Low class housing, 4 = Medium class housing, 5 = High class housing

The Concentric Ring Model   *The Sector Model*   *A typical British city*

Settlement

CBD (Central Business District) – this is where land is at its most expensive. A modernized city centre contains high rise office blocks, covered shopping arcades and pedestrianized streets. No houses are found here and there is little open space.

Inner city – around the CBD is an area of the town that was built in the last century. It is usually an area of industrial decline with high density terraced housing built to house factory workers. Many factories and older houses have now been demolished and the land redeveloped.

Inner suburbs – a residential area with many of the houses built during the 1920s and 1930s.

Outer suburbs – the newest part of the town with mixed land use. Included here would be new housing estates, council estates, out-of-town shopping areas, modern industrial parks and open space.

Greenbelt – an area around the city boundary where planning controls limit development.

There are many problems associated with living in the modern city:

- high crime rates
- high levels of unemployment
- poor air quality and other forms of pollution
- traffic congestion
- poor housing quality and urban decay
- areas of ethnic segregation which sometimes lead to violence and unrest.

As a result of these problems many people are moving out of the city into the surrounding countryside. The population of many cities is falling.

Cities in developing countries differ in a number of ways, as shown in the diagram below.

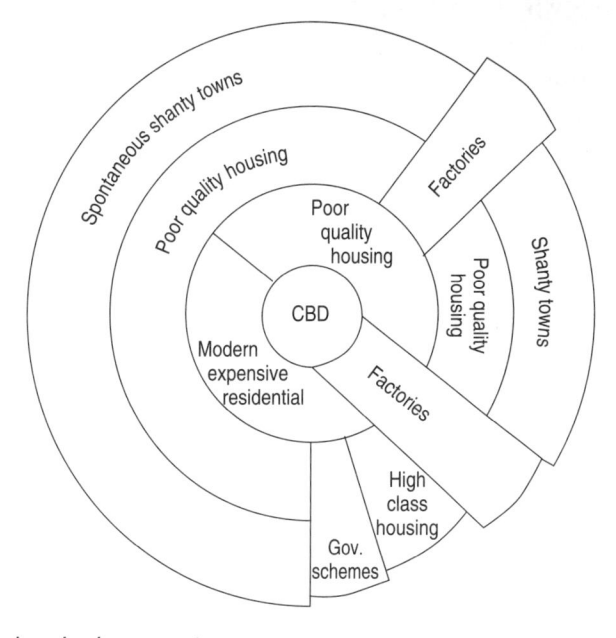

A typical city in a developing country

Most of these cities are growing rapidly due to push and pull factors:

- difficulties in subsistence agriculture mean food production does not meet demand
- people are attracted to cities to look for work and in the hope of raising their standards of living.

New arrivals face many problems when they get to the city. They have no money, no job and nowhere to live. They are forced to settle in spontaneous shanty towns on the edge of the city. In shanty towns housing is of poor quality, built of wood, corrugated iron or even cardboard. There is no running water or sanitation so diseases such as typhoid and dysentery are common. There are few job opportunities and there is tremendous strain on social and family life.

REVISION SUMMARY

If you need to revise this subject more thoroughly, see the relevant topics in the *Letts* GCSE *Geography Study Guide*.

6 Settlement

QUESTIONS

1 (a) Study Fig. 1 below. It is a model of the layout of a city in the developing world.

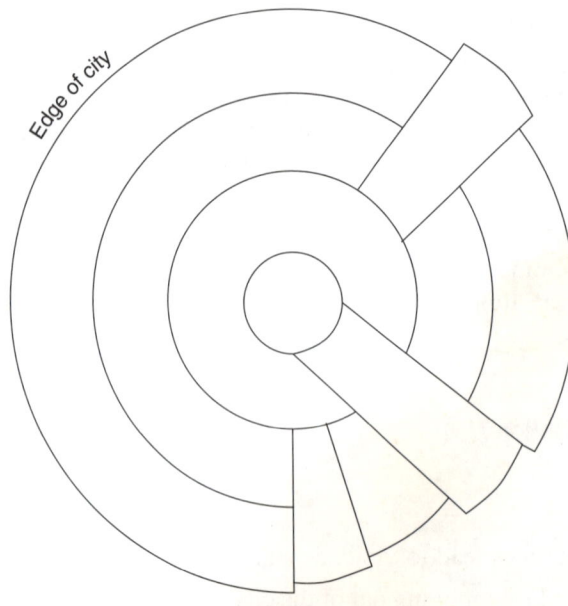

(i) Mark **each** of the following on Fig. 1. Use the letters in the brackets.

A large shopping centre with tall office blocks. (**O**)
An area where modern factories have been built along roads. (**F**)
An area where squatters have built shanty towns. (**S**)
An area where you would find expensive, high rise flats. (**H**)
(4)

Fig. 1

(ii) Give **two** reasons why people live in shanty towns. (2)

(iii) Give **two** reasons why many of the buildings in the Central Business District are tall with many storeys. (2)

(b) Study the OS map extract provided on page 50, scale 1:50 000.

(i) **Using map evidence only**, give **three** reasons for the site and growth of Keswick. (3)

(ii) A new road (part of the A66(T)) has been built to by-pass Keswick. Suggest **two** reasons why the by-pass was necessary. (2)

(iii) Using the OS map provided, measure the distance along the by-pass (A66(T)) from the western edge of the map (240235) to the bridge over the dual carriageway at the map reference 278240. Give your answer in kilometres. (1)

(iv) Listed below are some of the people who live in and around Keswick. Choose **three** and state whether you think they would be for or against the by-pass. In **each** case give **one** reason for your answer. (3)

A retired couple living in Keswick.
A shopkeeper in Keswick.
A farmer over whose land the by-pass was built.
A conservationist.

(v) State **three** improvements which could be made to the road system within a town such as Keswick to help speed up the traffic flow at peak periods. (3)

(c) Study Fig. 2 on page 29. It shows changes in the village of Braithwaite, situated three kilometres west of Keswick, between 1925 and 1985.

Settlement 6

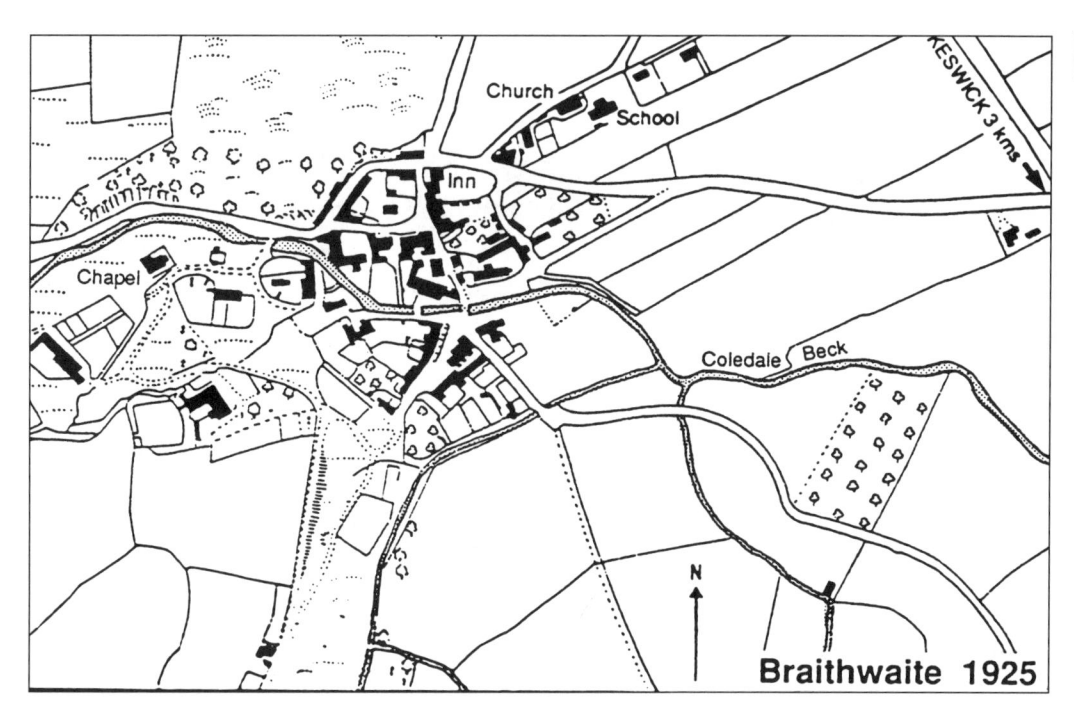

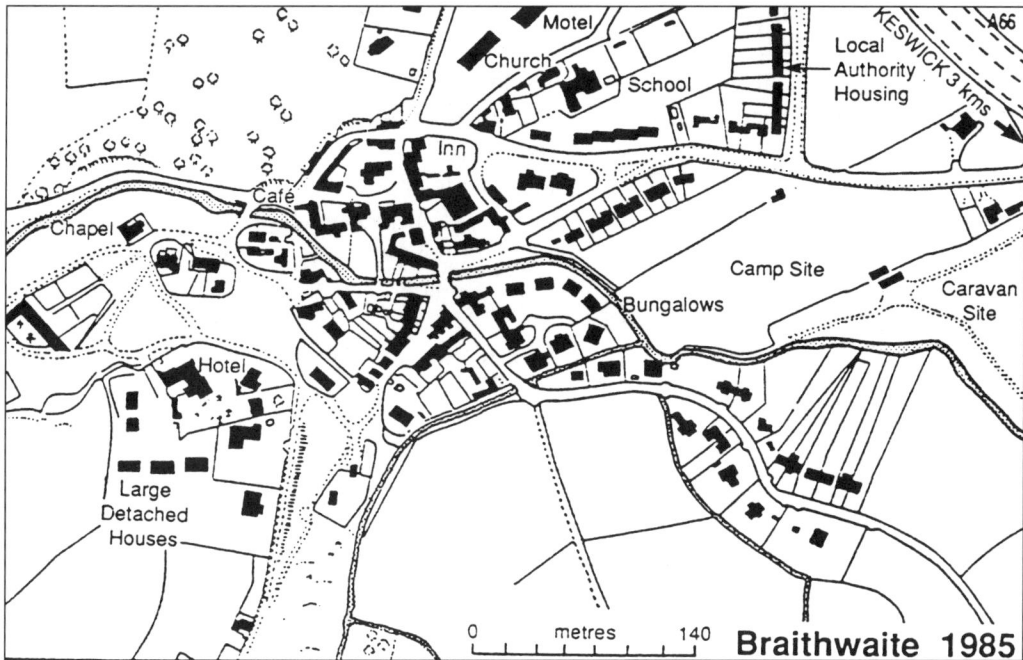

QUESTIONS

Fig. 2 Changes in village character

(i) People who live in Braithwaite work in Keswick and other towns in the area. What name is given to this type of village? (1)

(ii) The type of houses in Braithwaite changed between the 1920s and the 1980s. State **two** changes. (2)

(iii) What evidence is there on Fig. 2 that Braithwaite has developed a tourist industry in recent years? (2)

MEG 1993

7 Agriculture – specifically dairying

REVISION SUMMARY

Some farmers grow only crops (arable) while other farmers keep only animals (pastoral). Many of the farmers in the UK do a bit of both (mixed).

A CLOSER LOOK AT DAIRY FARMING

Dairying is a very important type of farming in Britain, but it cannot take place in all areas. In order to produce the maximum amount of milk dairy cows require certain conditions.

- The land has to be quite low and quite flat. Large animals such as cows find it difficult to climb steep slopes.
- The soil has to be deep and fertile with a large proportion of clay in it.
- The weather has to be wet with the rainfall spread evenly throughout the year.
- Temperatures have to be mild in winter (so the grass has a longer season in which to grow, cutting down the amount of winter feed needed) and cool in the summer (a hot, dry summer would dry out the grass, cause cows to perspire a lot and thus cut down the amount of milk produced).
- The farm should be fairly close to major towns and cities where milk can be sold, although nowadays this is less important as refrigerated lorries can keep milk fresh for longer.

PROBLEMS FACING DAIRY FARMERS

During the 1960s and early 1970s, under the European Community's Common Agricultural Policy, farmers were encouraged to produce as much food as they could. Whatever they produced would be bought. This policy, along with increased efficiency, has led to overproduction and the creation of 'butter, grain and beef mountains' as well as a 'wine lake'. In an effort to cut down the amount of milk produced, the EC introduced **dairy quotas** in 1984. A quota is a limit on how much each individual farmer is allowed to produce. Most farmers have been given a quota for less milk than they previously produced. A heavy fine is imposed if they exceed their quota.

Dairy farmers were faced with a problem: they had too much land, too many cows and were producing too much milk. Many had invested in new machinery and new buildings which had meant borrowing money from the banks. The problem they faced was how were they going to make enough money to make a profit.

This has forced many farmers into **diversification** to make ends meet. Diversification means producing some other crop or using the land in other ways. For example:

- growing cereals, or keeping some other animals such as sheep
- attracting tourists by converting farm buildings to holiday cottages or renting out fields as camp sites
- offering educational visits, such as nature trails or farm demonstrations
- providing sporting activities, such as pony trekking, mountain biking or golf driving ranges
- growing pick-your-own-fruit, which is very risky but in a good year can bring in a large profit.

THE ROLE OF THE GOVERNMENT

The government, through the Common Agricultural Policy, is now having a greater influence on what a farmer produces. By offering large subsidies (payments) farmers are being encouraged to change their farming practice. One such scheme is called **set-aside**. This is where a farmer receives a payment (about £200 for every hectare) for not farming part of his land – leaving it fallow. The field reverts back to a natural state. The advantages are that this option costs the farmer no money at all and it helps to cut food mountains.

FARMERS AND THE ENVIRONMENT

Modern farming techniques have had a profound effect on the environment. Over-use of artificial fertilizers, the spraying of pesticides and herbicides, the digging up of hedgerows, farm waste seeping into water courses and soil erosion are just some of the ways in which farming has had an adverse effect on the environment. Some farmers are now thinking more carefully about their farming methods and are paying more attention to the environment.

If you need to revise this subject more thoroughly, see the relevant topics in the Letts GCSE Geography Study Guide.

Letts Q&A

Agriculture – specifically dairying 7

1 (a) Study Fig. 1.

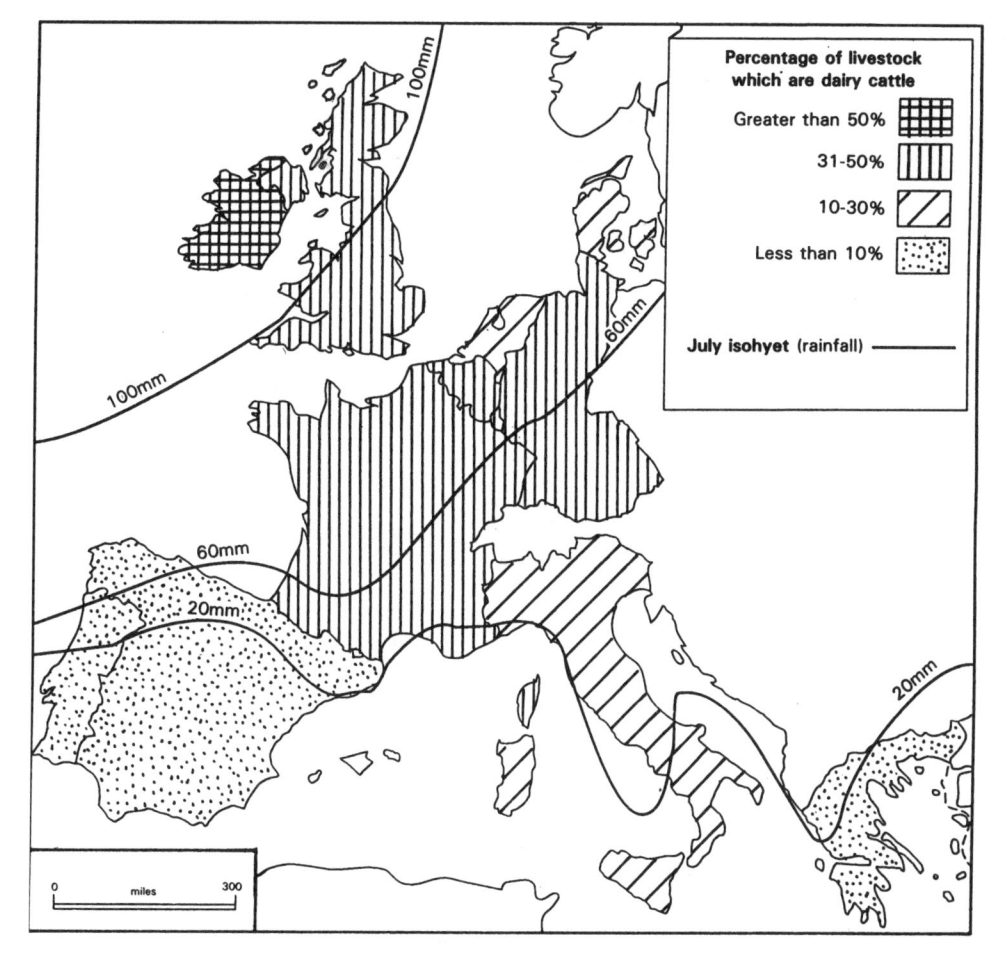

Fig. 1 Rainfall and dairy cattle

   (i) Describe the general pattern of percentage dairy cattle shown on the map. (1)

   (ii) What is the general relationship between the rainfall during July and the percentage of dairy cattle? (1)

   (iii) List ways in which the climate of southern Europe explains the low numbers of dairy cattle. (2)

(b) Study Fig. 2 on page 32.

   (i) Give **one** full reason why the field marked Y is most suitable for dairy farming. (2)

   (ii) Underline the correct answer to this statement. (1)

   As the farmer travels from the farmhouse to the field marked X he would go

   uphill all the way   downhill then uphill   downhill all the way   uphill then downhill

7 Agriculture – specifically dairying

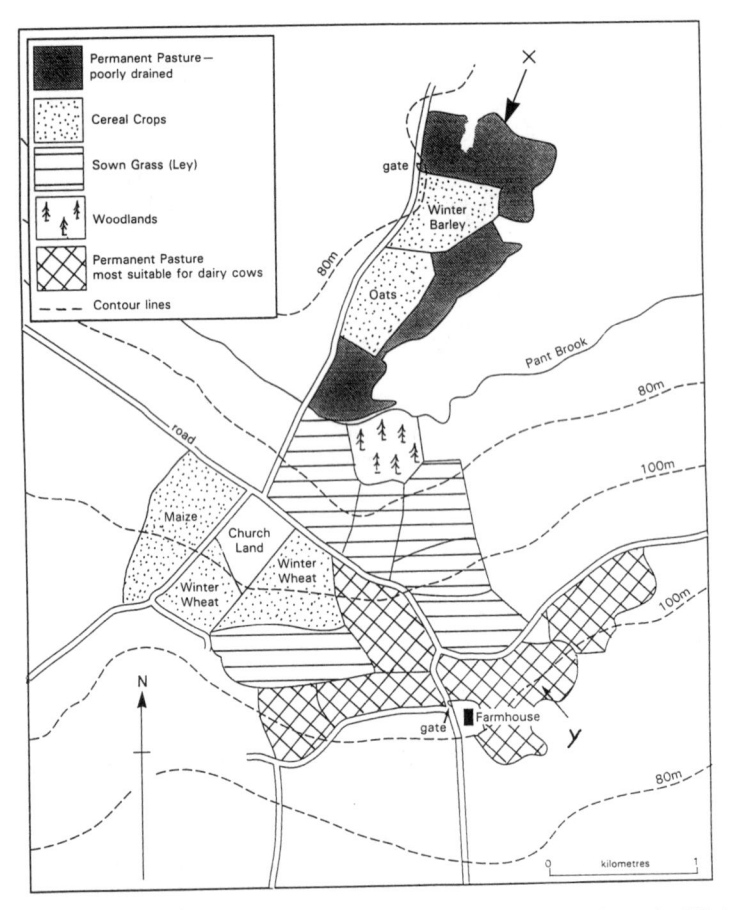

QUESTIONS

Fig. 2 Land use on Coed Morgan Farm – a dairy farm in Wales

(iii) 1. What is the distance (in kilometres) by road from the farmhouse gate to the gate in the field marked X? (1)

2. Describe two problems this could create for the farmer. (2)

(iv) 1. What is meant by the term permanent pasture? (1)

2. Give reasons to explain its location on this farm. (2)

(v) Although this is a dairy farm, the farmer grows other crops. Explain **two** reasons why he would do this. (4)

(c) Since 1984 dairy farmers have been greatly affected by quotas.

(i) What is a dairy quota? (1)

(ii) Give **one** reason why they were introduced. (2)

(iii) Describe **two** problems dairy farmers have faced as a result of quotas. (4)

(d) The government and conservationists are encouraging farmers to farm their land in more 'environmentally friendly' ways. Describe one or more of these ways. (You may like to consider organic farming, set-aside schemes or replanting of hedgerows.) (6)

WJEC 1992

Manufacturing industry 8

REVISION SUMMARY

In industry, to manufacture means to make something in a factory. Each factory can be looked at using a systems approach. **Costs of production** and the **raw materials** that go into the factory would be the **inputs**, jobs done in the factory would be the **processes** and the **finished products**, which the factory sells, would be its **outputs**.

INDUSTRIAL LOCATION

There are many things a company must consider before deciding where the best location for their business would be. Locational factors include:

- the site – is a large or small area of land needed and is it flat?
- raw materials – are they light or heavy and bulky? Do large amounts need to be imported?
- market – is it close, is it local or global?
- labour – is there an adequate supply? Is there skilled labour available?
- transport – are links to markets good?
- capital – is there enough money available?
- incentives – are grants, tax-free benefits or low rents available for certain areas?
- agglomeration – would it be an advantage to locate close to companies producing a similar product?
- inertia – perhaps it is more expensive to relocate than stay put.

There is no perfect location for a factory. After considering all the factors, the final decision will represent the best compromise location.

HOW INDUSTRY USES LAND

The amount of land needed by a factory depends very much on what is being made. During the nineteenth and early twentieth centuries, industry in Britain was dominated by 'heavy industry'. This included iron and steel, shipbuilding, textiles and heavy engineering. Works such as these require large expanses of land. They were located close to coal fields as coal was the only source of power. They were dirty and pollution was very much a problem. Today, much of this heavy industry has gone and has been replaced by 'lighter', non-polluting industries which require much smaller areas of land. Electricity is easily transported across the country so factories are no longer tied to a power source. This allows some industries to be '**footloose**', i.e. they are not dependent on one factor and so are free to locate where they want.

INDUSTRIAL CHANGE IN BRITAIN

Significant changes have occurred in the location of British industry during the last 50 years.

- Heavy industry has declined to be replaced by lighter industries.
- Fewer people are employed in manufacturing – more people now work in the tertiary sector (services).
- There has been a shift from inner city locations to more accessible edge-of-city sites.
- The government has had an increasing influence in where industry locates.

The consequences of these changes have been that:

- the traditional areas, such as the north-east, the north-west and south Wales, have declined in importance. It has been difficult to attract alternative industries owing mainly to the unattractive, blighted industrial landscape. High unemployment levels have resulted and a general migration of population out of these areas.
- modern industry now looks to locate on industrial estates close to motorways. The south-east, especially along the M4 corridor, has seen a significant growth in industry.
- less emphasis is placed now on employment in manufacturing. The tertiary sector now employs nearly twice as many people as the manufacturing sector.

If you need to revise this subject more thoroughly, see the relevant topics in the *Letts* GCSE *Geography Study Guide*.

8 Manufacturing industry

QUESTIONS

1 (a) Study the diagram below.

THE MANUFACTURE OF IRON AND STEEL

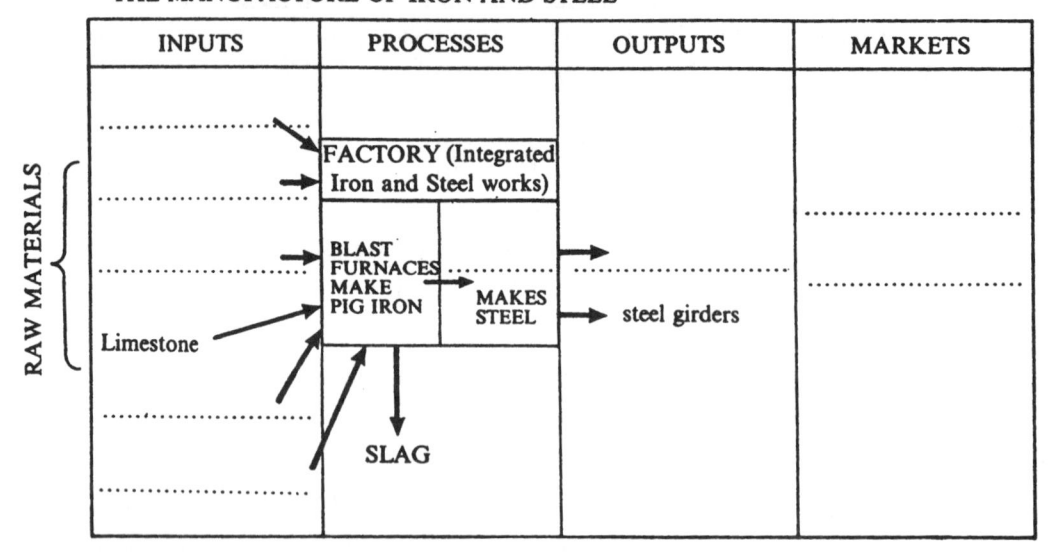

Put the following words in the correct places on the diagram.

electricity   car industry   iron ore   capital   coking coal
skilled workforce   steel sheets   shipbuilding   steel mill   (9)

(b) Study the diagram below. It shows factors which influence the location of a factory.

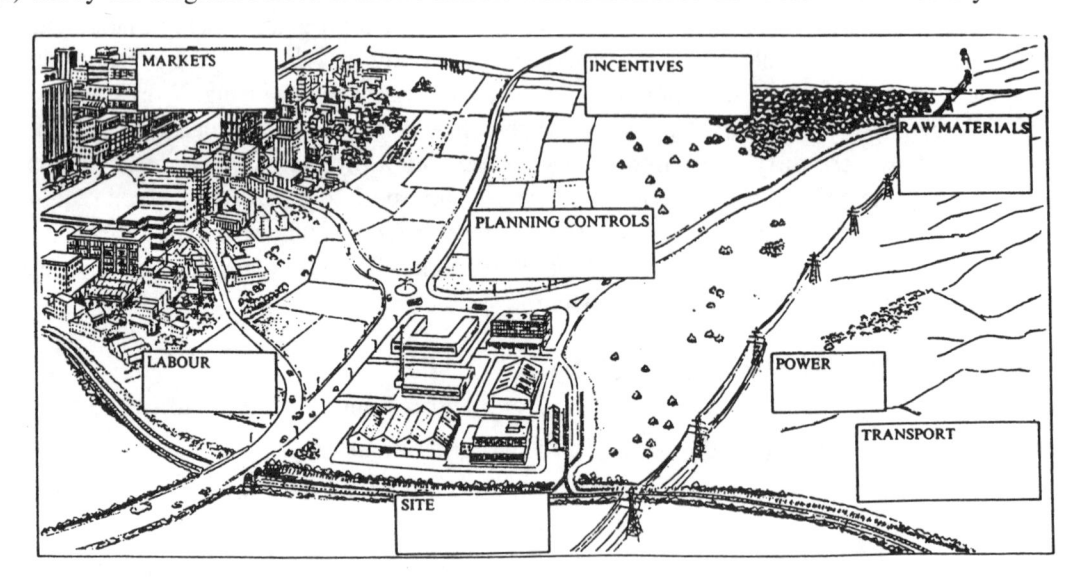

Choose **five** of the factors shown in the boxes on the diagram. Explain how they would be important when locating a factory. You should refer to industries which you have studied.

An example is shown below to help you.

- **Water** is very important for cooling in processes such as power generation. It is also used in processing – for example, in dyeing in the textile industries. Some industries such as brewing need clean water to make a good quality product.

(9)

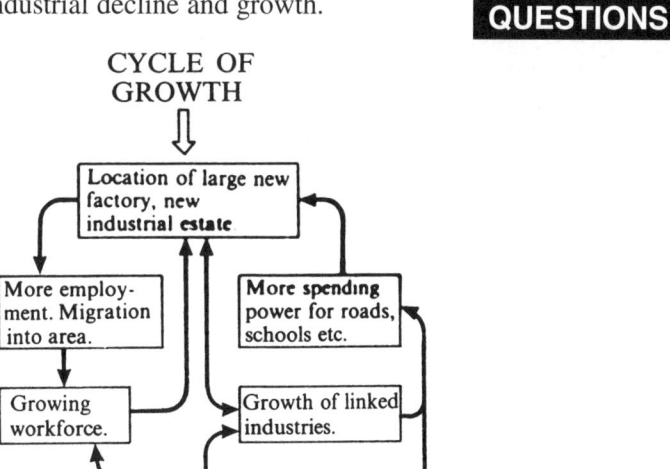

(c) Study the diagrams below. They show cycles of industrial decline and growth.

CYCLE OF DECLINE

- Closure of one or several large industries in area.
- Causes job loss. People leave area.
- Less money for councils to spend.
- Loss of skilled workers.
- Collapse of some linked industries.
- Less demand for services.
- Less money collected from taxes.
- Decline in services e.g. shops.
- Wealth of local area declines. Less investment.

CYCLE OF GROWTH

- Location of large new factory, new industrial estate
- More employment. Migration into area.
- More spending power for roads, schools etc.
- Growing workforce.
- Growth of linked industries.
- Increased demand for services.
- More taxes.
- More service industries.
- Increased wealth in area. More investment.

Choose an area that you have studied which shows **either** the effects of industrial decline **or** the effects of industrial growth.

Name your chosen area.

(i) Describe the decline **or** growth.

(ii) State reasons for the decline **or** growth.

(iii) Using your own knowledge and the information shown on the diagram above, describe the social and economic effects of the decline **or** growth you have described.

(iv) Explain what effects the decline **or** growth has had on the environment of your named area. (12)

NEAB 1992

9 Retailing

REVISION SUMMARY

Retailing is the selling of goods to the customer. A **consumer** is someone who buys goods from a shop. **Low order, convenience** goods, such as bread, milk and newspapers, are bought on a daily basis. Usually people would not be prepared to travel far in order to purchase such items. **Middle order, comparison** goods, such as shoes and clothes, are bought less frequently. Consumers compare prices and styles before deciding which items to buy. **High order, luxury** goods, such as jewellery and furniture, are only bought occasionally. Usually people are prepared to make a special journey and to travel further in order to purchase high order goods.

The **range** of an item or service is the maximum distance people would be prepared to travel in order to purchase that item or to obtain that particular service. The lower the order, the shorter the range. The **threshold** of an item or service is the minimum number of customers needed in order to make a profit. The higher the order, the greater the threshold.

Shops can be placed in a hierarchy depending on the types of goods they sell. Each shop should be sited at a location that best suits the type of goods they sell. A good location could lead to many customers and a healthy profit. A poor location could mean a business would struggle to survive.

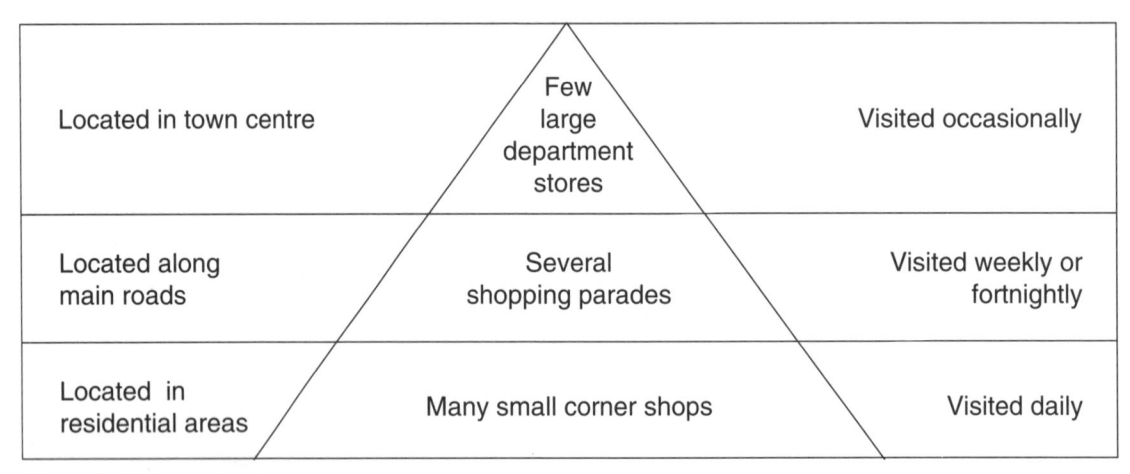

Located in town centre	Few large department stores	Visited occasionally
Located along main roads	Several shopping parades	Visited weekly or fortnightly
Located in residential areas	Many small corner shops	Visited daily

Shopping hierarchy in a town

TYPES OF SHOP

Corner shops – these are located within walking distance of people's homes. They sell low order, convenience goods and are open for long hours, e.g. 7 a.m. to 10 p.m. for example. They cater for people who work late or for those who have forgotten or run out of something. The corner shop is often the hub of the community with many customers known personally to the shop owner.

Shopping parade – here 5–15 shops are found in the suburbs, usually along main roads. They sell a mixture of comparison goods and convenience goods. There may be several **specialist shops**, such as a bakery, a chemist and maybe a Post Office.

Large department store – found in the centre of the town. It offers a wide range of high order goods in different departments, such as TVs and videos in the electrical department, furniture and maybe even carpets. People are prepared to make a special journey in order to visit the shop.

Superstore – a modern development. A large shop, over 2500 m^2, found on the outskirts of the town. Superstores, such as Sainsbury and Tesco, have been attracted to edge-of-city locations as:

- they are near main roads, giving easy access for both customers and delivery lorries
- land is cheaper
- there is plenty of space to build a large store plus room for car parking and for lorries to turn
- the congestion of the town is avoided.

Superstores attract customers by:

- staying open late

Retailing 9

- selling products at a cheaper price than smaller shops (they can do this because they sell goods in bulk)
- offering free car parking and cheaper petrol
- providing a coffee shop and/or cafeteria.

RECENT TRENDS IN SHOPPING

Shopping is a major growth activity in Britain today. In the past shops were always located in the town centre. People moved from shop to shop, along crowded pavements as traffic rolled past on the main road. Very little thought was given to the needs of the shopper and shopping was considered to be a necessary evil. Today many town centres have been pedestrianized with trees, benches and fountains. Town centres have been forced to make these changes in direct response to the growth of out-of-town shopping areas. There is competition for customers and people will shop where the shopping is made more attractive. Superstores, hypermarkets and even large shopping malls are now found on the edge of many towns. Shopping habits have changed for the following reasons:

- refrigeration and domestic freezers mean food can be kept fresh for longer
- more people work and do not have the time to shop as frequently
- the number and range of pre-prepared 'ready meals' has increased
- people are prepared to travel further to shop as car ownership has increased
- being paid monthly means that people find it more convenient to buy in bulk
- increased affluence has created a demand for more luxury items.

REVISION SUMMARY

If you need to revise this subject more thoroughly, see the relevant topics in the *Letts* GCSE *Geography Study Guide*.

9 Retailing

QUESTIONS

1 (a) Study the map extract on page 51 which shows part of North Yorkshire.

(i) List **three** different services that can be found in the town of Settle that are shown on the map. (3)

(ii) Use the map to explain why Settle has become the largest town in this area of North Yorkshire. (3)

(iii) There are plans to build a new superstore in Settle at the location marked **X** on the map. Describe the site of the superstore in relation to the town of Settle. (3)

(b) Study Fig. 1 below.

Settlement	Number of different types of shops				
	General Store	Post Office	Newsagent	Gift Shops	Electrical Shops
Settle	5	1	4	4	2
Stainforth	1	1	1	0	0
Langcliffe	1	1	0	0	0
Helwith Bridge	1	0	0	0	0

Fig. 1 A sample of shops found in the Settle area

(i) Use the information in Fig. 1 to complete the bar graph below.

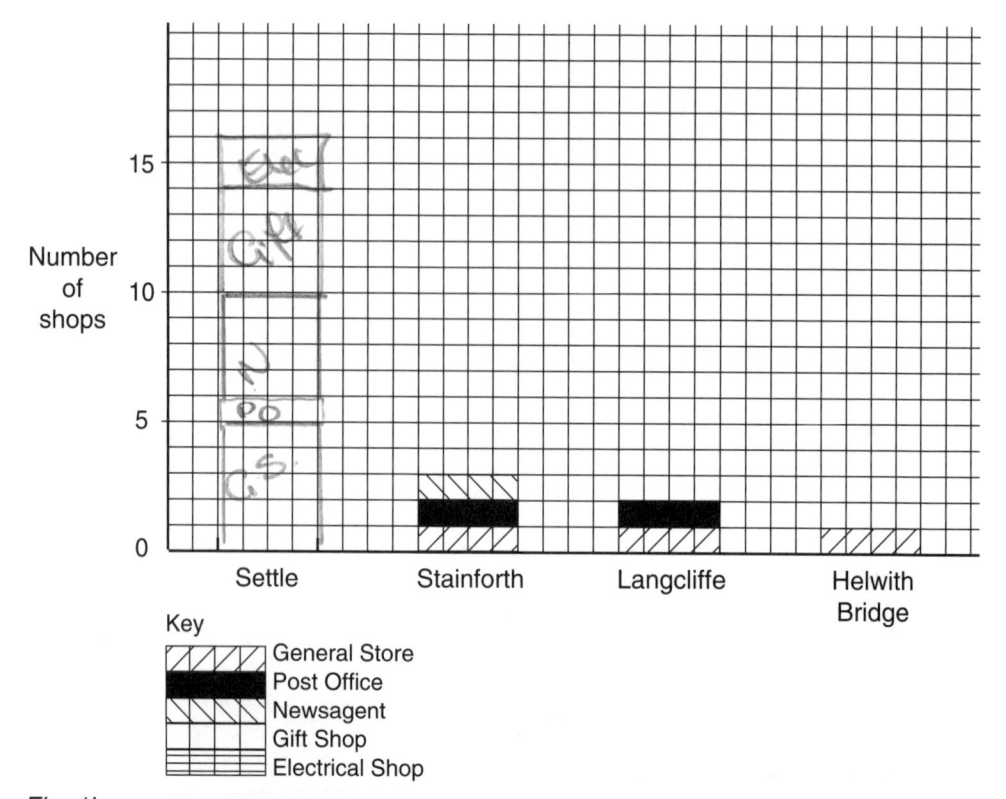

Fig. 1b

(ii) Describe the pattern of shops in the four settlements as shown by Fig. 1. (3)

(iii) Explain why **gift shops and electrical shops** are located in Settle. (2)

(iv) In what ways would Fig. 1 be different if the survey had been carried out twenty years ago? (2)

(c) Read the extract below.

> Plans have been submitted for the building of a new superstore in the town of Settle in North Yorkshire.
> The settlement provides an ideal location. The threshold population needed for a store of this size can be found within a 40 km radius. Normally, it is not expected that customers will travel this far to such a superstore. However, surveys have shown that the range in this area of rural North Yorkshire is a much longer distance than is usual. The store would therefore easily be viable.

Fig. 2. Report on the suitability of Settle as a location for a new superstore

(i) Explain the meaning of the underlined terms in the article. (3)

(ii) Describe **two** ways in which the customer will be disadvantaged by shopping in this superstore rather than in many of the smaller shops in Settle. (2)

(d) The people of Stainforth, a village four kilometres to the north of Settle, have written to the local council objecting to the planned superstore. Suggest why they have done this and what they might have said. (6)

WJEC 1990

10 Tourism and leisure

REVISION SUMMARY

Tourism is the industry that caters for people who want a holiday. Over 70% of people living in the UK took some kind of holiday in 1993, though for some it was just a day trip. Tourism is a major industry, providing 18 million jobs for people across Europe. Places people visit for a holiday are called resorts. The tourist industry has grown rapidly over the last thirty years. This is because:

- people have more leisure time owing to working shorter hours, having paid leave from their work or retiring at a younger age
- people have become wealthier, so they have more money to spend on luxuries such as holidays
- more information is available about other places so people want to visit them
- it is easier to get to places that were once considered far away
- a full range of purpose-built resorts and package holidays has become available.

There are many different types of holiday, for example:

- **long stay summer resorts**. These attract people who want to spend a week or more in one centre. They are usually found on the coast next to sandy beaches, e.g. the countries around the Mediterranean Sea. Tourists are attracted by the warm, dry, sunny weather, excellent beaches and a warm sea to swim in, bars, night-clubs, discos and other beachside facilities, a variety of good standard accommodation which caters for families with young children, and the fact that most of the resorts can be reached easily, being only two to four hours flying time away. A **package holiday** is where one payment is made and the tour operator arranges the flight, accommodation, airport transfers, meals and entertainment.

  Despite the lure of the Mediterranean, most British holiday-makers take their summer holiday in Britain. The most popular destinations are the south coast and south-west of England where the weather is usually better. Many British holiday resorts now offer a full range of facilities that cater for the whole family, especially attractions that do not depend on hot, sunny weather.

- **long haul** holidays are becoming more popular. This is where tourists travel long distances to far away, exotic places such as Australia and New Zealand, Africa, the Far East or the Caribbean. Many developing countries, such as Kenya and The Gambia, are trying to expand their tourist industry. They see it as a means of improving their economy.

- **short stay attractions.** These are usually visited by people on day trips or on short breaks. These places have to be easy to reach. Included here are towns which are known for their culture, history or art. In Britain, a popular destination for a short break or day trip is one of the eleven **National Parks**. These are areas of 'outstanding natural beauty' which have been set aside for special protection. Each National Park Authority has to protect and enhance the landscape, carefully manage the economic activities that take place in the park, e.g. farming, forestry, quarrying, help the public to participate in recreational activities, and give care and consideration to those people who live and work in the Park. Every year nearly 100 million visitors enjoy the scenic attraction of these diverse landscapes.

- **winter holidays.** Since the late 1970s winter sports holidays have become very popular. Areas such as the Alps have seen a large increase in the number of visitors. This has led to a huge growth in the skiing industry and in the number of tour operators offering skiing holidays. A number of purpose-built ski resorts have sprung up in response to the growing demand. Skiing is a very specialized activity and requires specialist facilities. Ski runs (pistes) have to be prepared, ski lifts installed, hotels built, medical facilities made available and a range of evening entertainment activities offered.

The influx of many tourists to an area can, in many cases, result in a **conflict** of interests. For example:

- **in coastal areas.** Around many parts of the Mediterranean, the building of holiday resorts has created an unbroken urban landscape. This has led to the clearing of the natural vegetation, the

Tourism and leisure

destruction of many wildlife habitats and has forced local farmers to move inland. Local resources, such as water, are often stretched to the limit.

Even in Britain, coastal environments are sensitive. For example, where sand dunes exist constant trampling can lead to severe wind erosion, walkers damage coastal paths and more tourists mean more noise, more litter and more pollution.

- **in National Parks.** Conflicts may arise over how best to use the land. There are many interested parties. For example, farmers may want to use more land at the expense of the Forestry Commission; the Ministry of Defence own large tracts of land that they use for military exercises; water companies may want to build more reservoirs; industry may want to extract natural resources such as rock in quarries; property developers may want to build new homes. There may even be conflict of interest between different groups of people who use the Park for leisure: water sports enthusiasts will disturb fishermen, horse riding may conflict with ramblers.

- **winter sports.** Mountain environments, such as the Alps, are very fragile. Large numbers of tourists attracted to the mountains to ski can seriously affect the delicately balanced ecosystem. Types of damage include:
  - bulldozing slopes for ski runs compacts the soil, reducing infiltration which leads to an increase in surface runoff. As a result, there is an increased risk of flooding and soil erosion is more likely. The threat of flooding is greater during spring when snow melt swells rivers **and** during summer when thunderstorms bring heavy rain.
  - providing tarmac areas for car parking has the same effect as above
  - removing trees increases the risk of avalanche
  - skiing down a mountain on a thin snow cover can damage delicate plants underneath.

REVISION SUMMARY

If you need to revise this subject more thoroughly, see the relevant topics in the *Letts* GCSE Geography Study Guide.

10 Tourism and leisure

QUESTIONS

1 (a) A family received these four postcards from their friends who had gone on holiday.

> **A** The weather is wonderful; not a cloud in the sky and the temperature is about 28 °C every day. The beach is lovely and sandy and there is a really great night life in the clubs and discos. Of course we have tasted the local wine!
>
> **B** It is very cold here, but we have had lots of sunshine. The snow is deep and crisp. We went walking on a glacier yesterday, and I saw a corrie and an arête, just like those we studied in Geography.
>
> **C** We have tried out lots of activities like abseiling, pot-holing and walking. The weather is cloudy and cool. The scenery is so wild and beautiful, with outcrops of grey-white rock. It is quite clear why this area became a National Park.
>
> **D** Our hotel is very modern. Temperatures are very high every day, so we are glad of the beautiful swimming pool. The scenery is spectacular but the people live in great poverty in the shanty towns and subsistence farming villages away from the resort area.

(a) (i) Five holiday resorts are marked on the map below, with boxes. **Four** of these places are described in the postcards.

Show which place is described in each of the postcards **by writing each letter, A, B, C and D, in its correct box on the map.** (4)

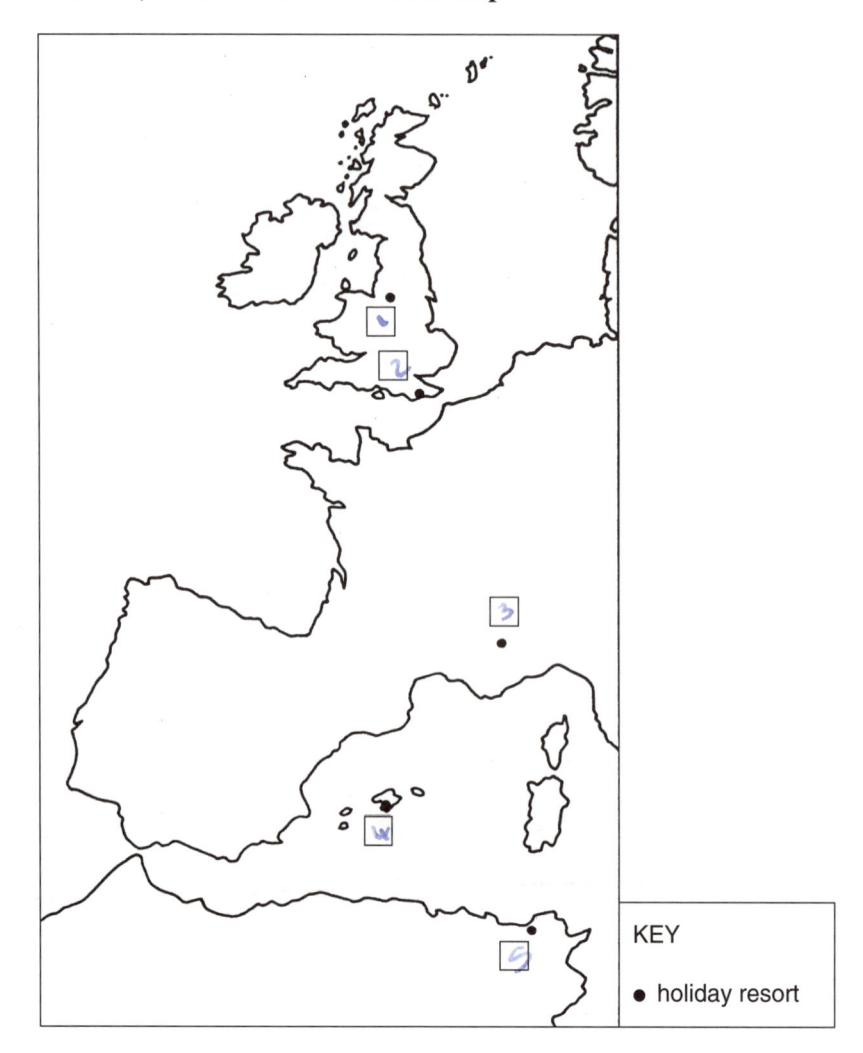

Tourism and leisure

(ii) Write a brief description of **either** a corrie **or** an arête. (2)

(iii) Postcard C was written from an area with some limestone scenery. How can you tell? (2)

(iv) Postcard C was written from a National Park. Give **one** of the main reasons why National Parks were set up in England and Wales. (2)

(v) Tourists can sometimes come into conflict with other landusers in the National Parks. Describe **two** ways that conflict can happen. (2)

(vi) A tourist industry can bring both advantages and disadvantages. Describe **some of** these advantages and disadvantages. Use places and examples you have studied. (6)

(b) Study the climate graph for a holiday resort in the French Alps.

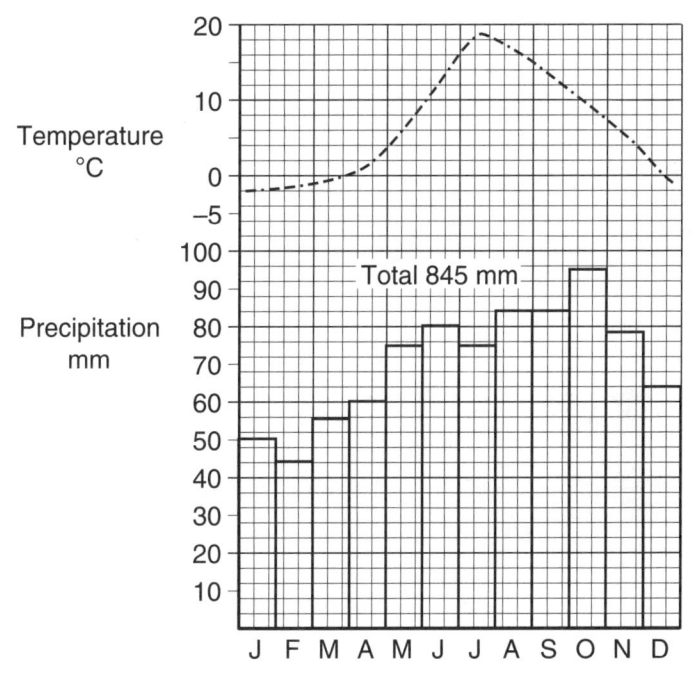

The climate of this area makes it popular for holiday makers from the United Kingdom. Explain why, using evidence from the graph. (3)

(c) Look at the photograph and the diagram on page 44. They show an Alpine resort.

(i) Describe both the natural tourist attractions **and** the man-made tourist attractions of the area shown above. (6)

(ii) Some people say that developing the ski industry in the Alps has damaged the environment. Suggest why. (3)

10 Tourism and leisure

QUESTIONS

Photo/map by permission of:
Thomson Tour Operations 1992

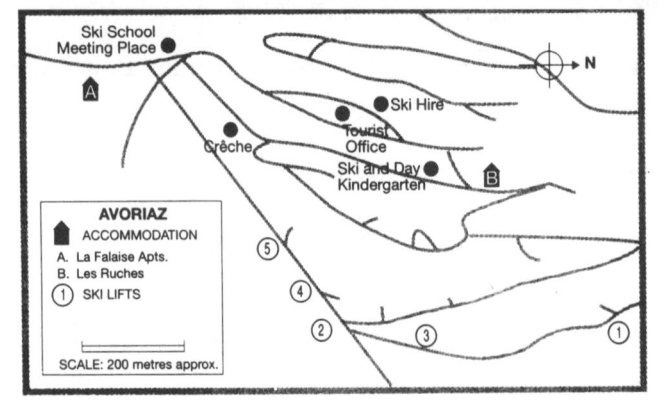

AVORIAZ
■ ACCOMMODATION
A. La Falaise Apts.
B. Les Ruches
① SKI LIFTS
SCALE: 200 metres approx.

NEAB 1993

Employment structures in developed and developing countries 11

REVISION SUMMARY

Industry can be classified into four sectors – primary, secondary, tertiary and quaternary.

- Industries in the **primary** sector extract minerals, crops and fish from the Earth's surface.
- Industries in the **secondary** sector use and/or process some of the products of primary industry and from them manufacture goods that people need, e.g. create cement from limestone, clay and gypsum.
- **Tertiary** industries provide back-up services. They include office work, retailing, entertainment, transport and financial services. Most of these are found in urban areas.
- **Quaternary** industries include the new hi-tech information services such as computer software. This is the industrial sector that has developed most recently.

The relative importance of each of these individual sectors changes as a country develops.

- A country at an early stage of industrial development is dominated by primary industry (farming and possibly mining). Such countries often export the primary products to the developed world. They may become dependent on one or two products, e.g. Nigeria on oil, Sudan on cotton, and be at the mercy of fluctuations in commodity prices.
- The next stage of development shows growth of employment in the secondary industrial sector, i.e. in manufacturing, and a decline in employment in the primary sector as primary industries become more mechanized or mineral resources begin to run out. Usually, among the first manufacturing industries to develop are the textile, footwear and food processing industries. They are reasonably labour intensive so take advantage of low wage rates, have a large internal market, have locally available raw materials and do not demand too much sophisticated equipment.
- As a country reaches a more advanced stage of development, the primary sector shrinks to a low level. The secondary sector also declines, but less so. The tertiary sector expands rapidly as service industries (administration, commercial, welfare, medical, tourist) develop.

CHARACTERISTICS OF DEVELOPING AND DEVELOPED COUNTRIES

Developing countries	Developed countries
High birth rate, falling death rate, so rapid population growth	Low birth rate, low death rate, usually population growth is slow
Nutrition often below level for good health	Generally good nutritional levels
Low doctor/nurse: population ratio	Many more doctors, nurses and hospitals
Literacy rates quite low	Literacy rates at a high level
Poorly developed communication networks	Dense road and rail networks
Lack investment capital so money borrowed from World Bank and countries in the developed world – some have massive debts	Money and know-how often invested in developing countries – many loans are still outstanding
Primary industries dominate, so low GNP (gross national product)	Secondary and tertiary sectors dominate, creating considerable wealth so high GNP
If at stage of manufacturing industrial growth, many people move from rural to urban areas, one result is shanty towns	In more advanced countries, major cities decline in population as people move to rural areas and commute to work
Most are in Africa, Asia and South America	Most are in Europe and North America

11 Employment structures in developed and developing countries

REVISION SUMMARY

TRIANGULAR GRAPHS AND SCATTER GRAPHS

The **triangular graph** is often used to show employment structure. At first glance it is not that easy to read. Study the example given below carefully. In this case:

A – Tanzania = 80% primary, 6% secondary, 14% tertiary
B – Italy = 14% primary, 43% secondary, 43% tertiary

Work out the readings for C, which is the UK.

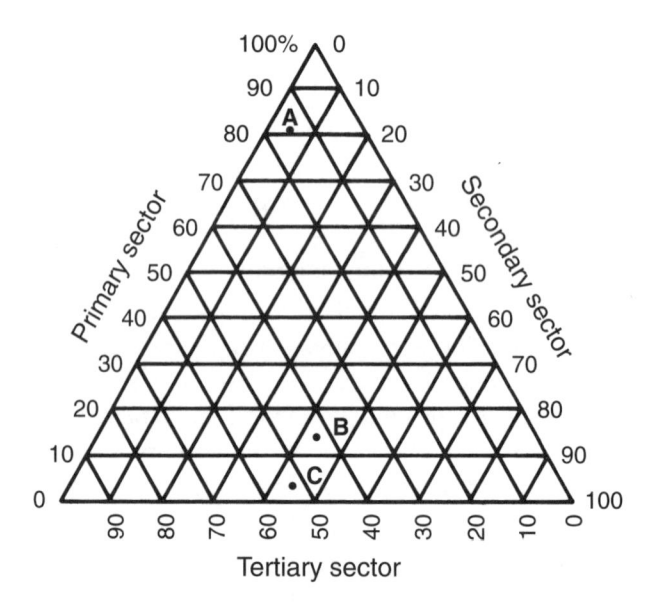

A **scatter graph** shows the relationship between two sets of geographical data. The set of data that is the cause of the other (the dependent) set is plotted along the horizontal axis.

In this case, the size of a settlement's population influences the number of services it has. The more strongly the points plotted on a scatter graph conform to a straight line, the stronger the relationship between the two sets of data.

If you need to revise this subject more thoroughly, see the relevant topics in the *Letts* GCSE *Geography Study Guide.*

Employment structures in developed and developing countries   11

QUESTIONS

1 (a) Study the table below. It shows employment structures in six countries.

	Percentage of workers in the		
1988	Primary sector %	Secondary sector %	Tertiary sector %
South Korea	20	30	50
United Kingdom	2	42	56
India	68	14	18
Ghana	54	20	26
Australia	5	33	62
Brazil	29	26	45

(i) What is meant by the:

1. Primary sector?

2. Secondary sector? (2)

(ii) Match each of these pie charts to one of the countries in the table. (2)

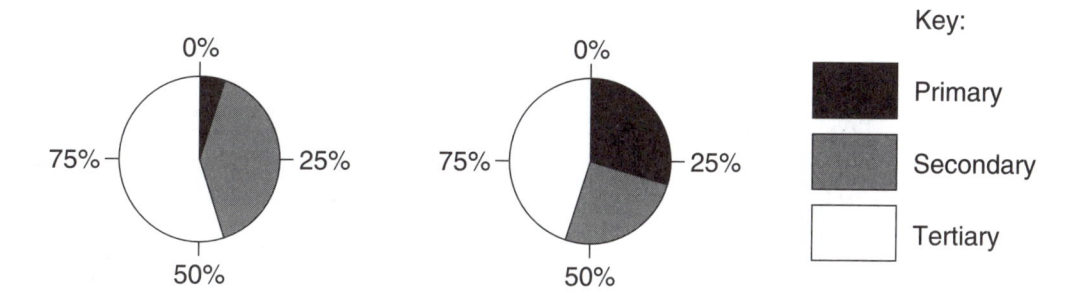

Key:
- Primary
- Secondary
- Tertiary

(iii) Use the information above to complete the table below. Place each of the six countries in the correct box. (3)

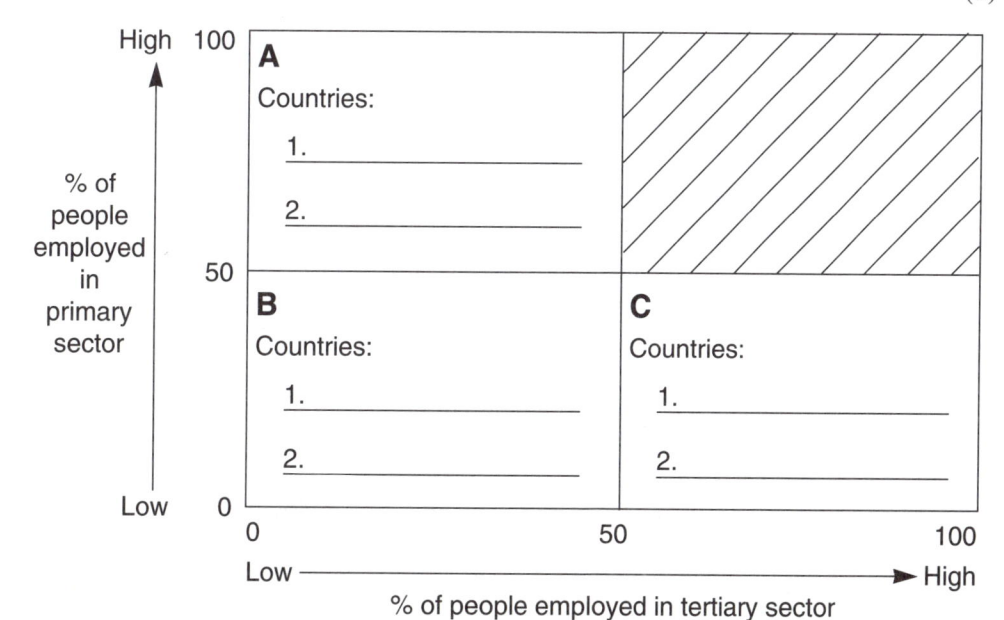

% of people employed in primary sector (Low 0 — High 100)

A
Countries:
1. _____
2. _____

B
Countries:
1. _____
2. _____

C
Countries:
1. _____
2. _____

% of people employed in tertiary sector (Low 0 — High 100)

11 Employment structures in developed and developing countries

QUESTIONS

(iv) The boxes are labelled **A, B** and **C**. Match the letters to the statements below.

'Economically **developing** countries'   =

'Economically **developed** countries'   =

'Newly industrialising countries'   =

(v) Give **two** characteristics of economically **developing** countries. Do not write about **industry and employment structure**. (2)

(b) Study the chart below. It gives information about industrial development in South Korea.

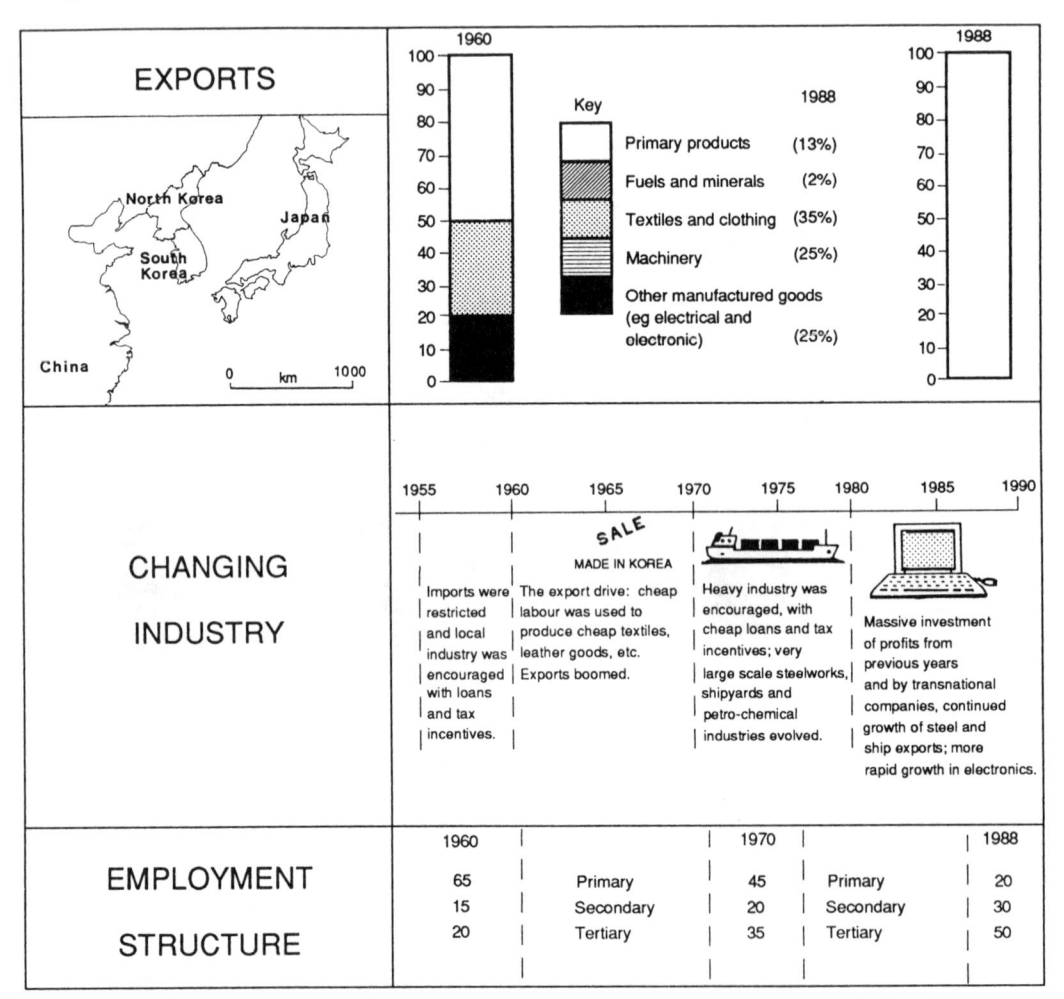

[Chart showing Exports (1960 and 1988), Changing Industry timeline 1955-1990, and Employment Structure]

Key (1988):
- Primary products (13%)
- Fuels and minerals (2%)
- Textiles and clothing (35%)
- Machinery (25%)
- Other manufactured goods (eg electrical and electronic) (25%)

Changing Industry:
- Imports were restricted and local industry was encouraged with loans and tax incentives.
- The export drive: cheap labour was used to produce cheap textiles, leather goods, etc. Exports boomed.
- Heavy industry was encouraged, with cheap loans and tax incentives; very large scale steelworks, shipyards and petro-chemical industries evolved.
- Massive investment of profits from previous years and by transnational companies, continued growth of steel and ship exports; more rapid growth in electronics.

Employment Structure:
	1960	1970	1988
Primary	65	45	20
Secondary	15	20	30
Tertiary	20	35	50

(i) Complete the graph of **exports** in 1988 (top right hand corner of chart) using the figures given in brackets on the chart above. (2)

(ii) List **two** ways in which the government encouraged the development of manufacturing. (2)

(iii) Which sector of the employment structure showed the **greatest** change between the 1960s and 1980s? (1)

(iv) Give **two** reasons to explain the changes in employment structure shown in the table. (4)

48

Employment structures in developed and developing countries

(v) Give **two** reasons to explain why textiles and clothing are often the first industries to be developed in an economically **developing** country. (4)

(vi) Suggest an economic and a social disadvantage which this rapid industrialization may have brought to South Korea. (4)

(c) **Case study**

Name an area in any part of the world where **either** industry **or** agriculture has declined. Describe the reasons for the decline and the effects on the people living there.

(i) Reasons for the decline (state whether answer refers to industry **or** agriculture).

(ii) Effects on people living there. (9)

MEG/WJEC 1994

2

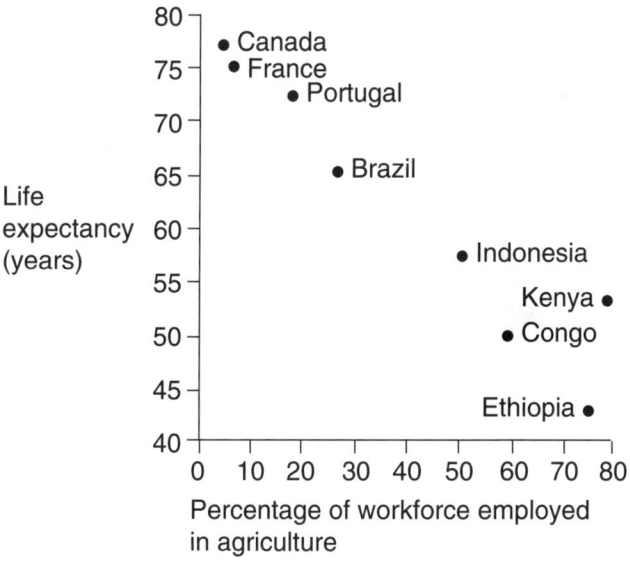

Reference diagram 1: life expectancy and percentage of workforce employed in agriculture in selected countries

(a) Look at reference diagram 1 above.

Describe the connection between life expectancy and employment in agriculture shown in the graph. (2)

(b) Explain why each of the following is a good measure of a country's level of development.

(i) Life expectancy

(ii) Percentage of workforce employed in agriculture (4)

SEB 1994

Map extract of Keswick. Scale 1:50 000.

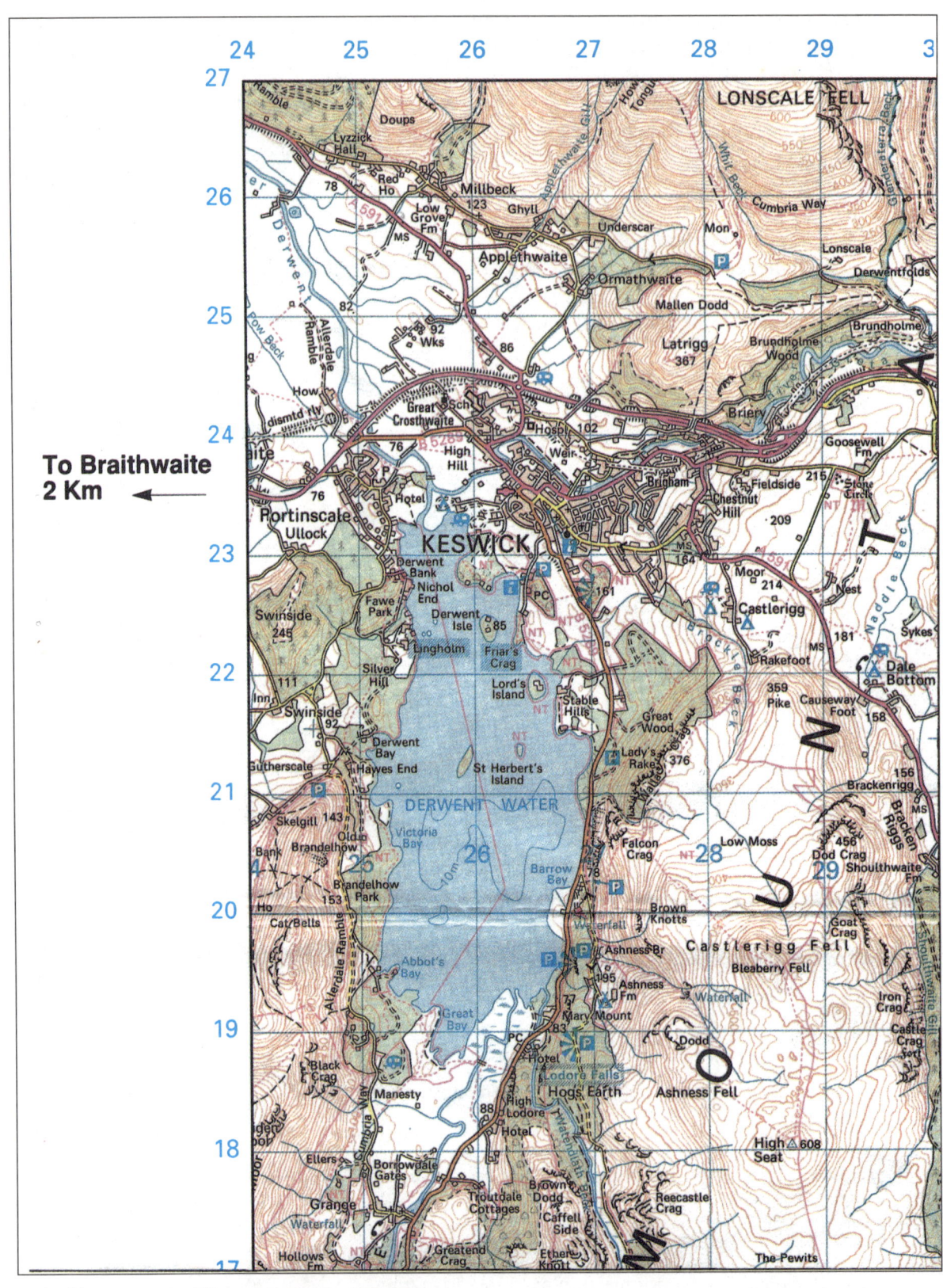

© Crown Copyright

Resource material for Question 1 (Unit 1) pp6–7 and Question 1 (Unit 6) p 28.

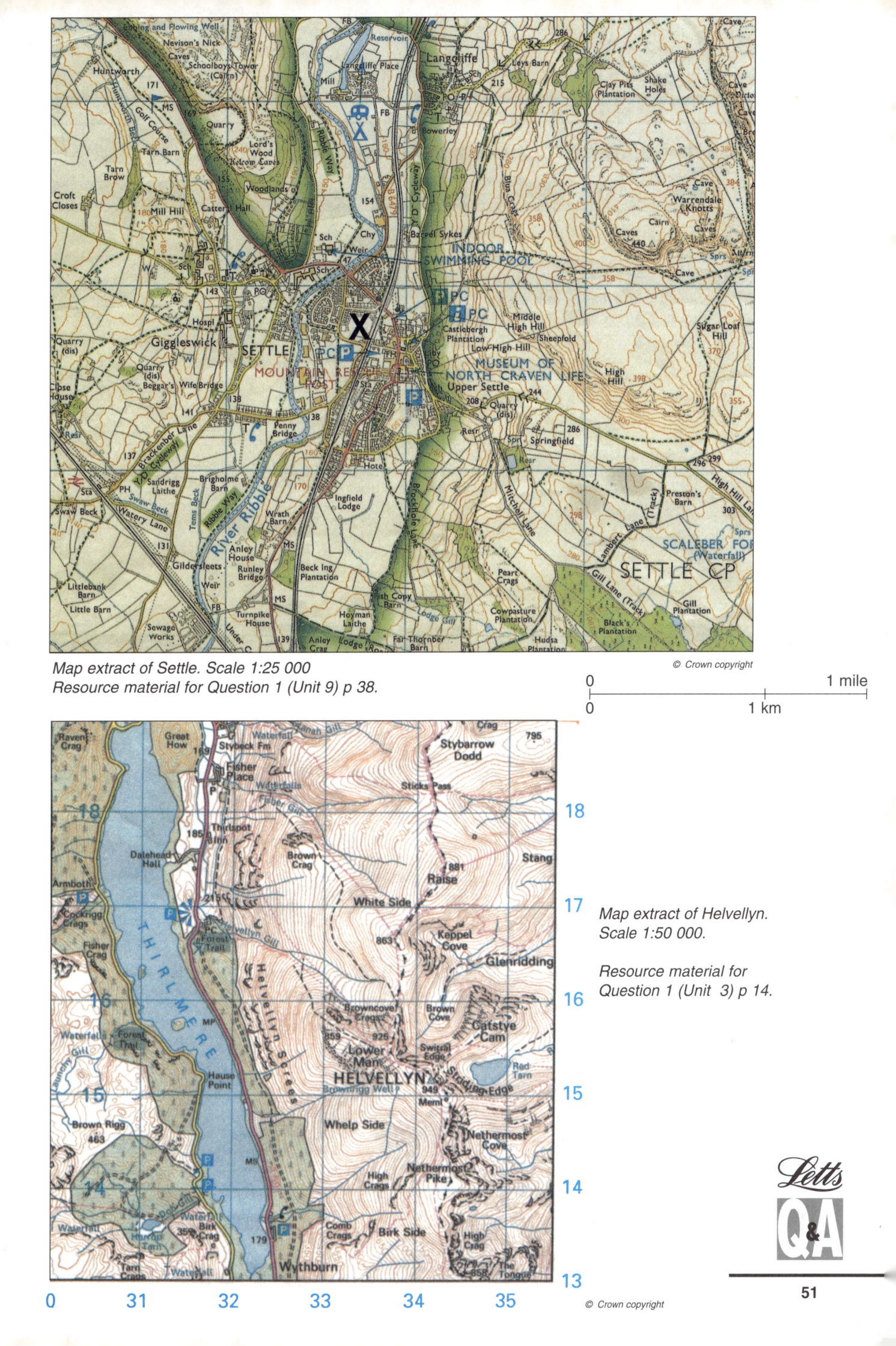

Map extract of Settle. Scale 1:25 000
Resource material for Question 1 (Unit 9) p 38.

© Crown copyright

0 ——————————— 1 mile
0 ——————————— 1 km

Map extract of Helvellyn.
Scale 1:50 000.

Resource material for
Question 1 (Unit 3) p 14.

Letts
Q&A

51

© Crown copyright

Answers

1 THE WATER CYCLE AND RIVERS AND THEIR VALLEYS

| Question | Answer | Mark |

1 (a) (i)

Examiner's tip Once you realize that evaporation is the conversion of water as a liquid into a gas – water vapour, which rises from the surface of the land (see vertical arrow on diagram) the sequence of the next three processes is clear.

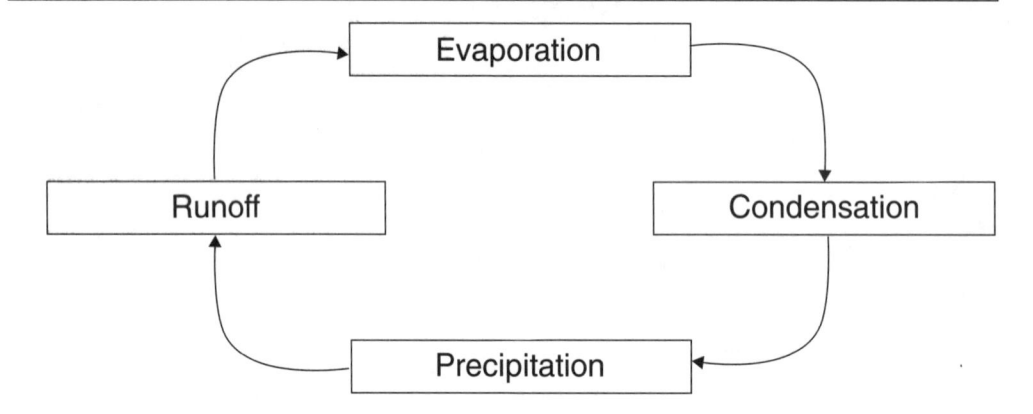

Evaporation → Condensation → Precipitation → Runoff → (Evaporation)

1

(ii) Transpiration 1

(iii) Because it is warmer in summer and higher temperatures lead to greater transpiration.
Alternatively, because there are more leaves on the trees in summer. 1

(iv) Water table 1

(b)

Examiner's tip This involves you in a study of an OS map extract. Make sure you are aware of the policy of your examination group. Will a key for all the symbols used on the map be supplied to you in the examination or will you be expected to know them?

(i) A confluence 1

(ii) The main features of the River Derwent are: a general NNW course; a very gentle gradient along the river; some meanders just after its exit from the lake for about 1 km; all its tributaries enter from the east; an ox bow lake. 3

(iii)

Examiner's tip When the phrase 'using map evidence only' is used in a question, it means just that. There is no point in including in your answer details that you have learned in class or from a textbook, if they are not evident on the map.

Answers to Unit 1

Question	Answer	Mark
	This is a lacustrine (lake) delta. It is an area of flat land, extending into the lake and it is quite marshy. The river flows through the middle of it.	3
(iv)	The River Derwent carries a large load (since it has just left the mountains). The velocity of the river water is checked as it flows into the lake. This leads to a loss of energy by the river. It is forced to deposit its load.	3
(c) (i)	Many river valleys have a flat floor which may be even lower than the river itself. When the river overflows, this flat land (flood plain) is flooded and the water has difficulty in returning to the river even when the river stops overflowing. The river bed may have risen through the river depositing its load on it, so there is less room for the river to rise before overflowing.	2
(ii)	The channel may be dredged, so it is made deeper to take more water. The material obtained through dredging may be piled up on the river banks to make a more effective barrier to flooding. (Alternatively, you could mention that straightening the river's course increases the velocity of the river, making flooding less likely.)	2
(d) (i)	(Name *one*) Ox bow lake or cut off (A) *OR* levees (B)	1

(ii)

Examiner's tip You cannot be expected to draw this cross-section to scale as the line X–Y provided is more than four times the distance on the diagram.

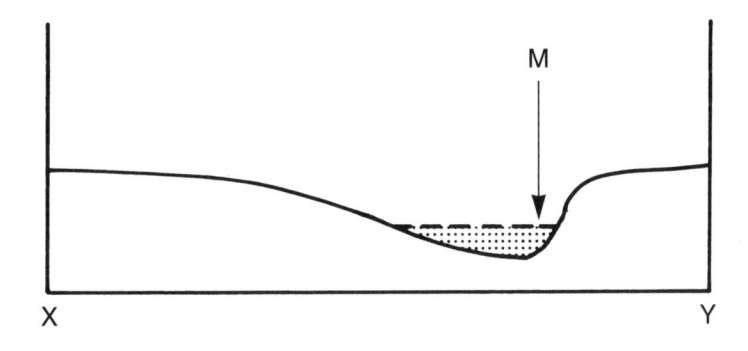

[Cross-section diagram showing valley profile from X to Y with point M marked by an arrow pointing to a depositional area]

2

(iii)

Examiner's tip Feature A is chosen here because, though an ox bow lake is a feature of little significance, it is popular with examiners because both river erosion and deposition occur in its formation. Usually one would use an annotated diagram when describing its formation.

Answers to Unit 1

Question	Answer	Mark

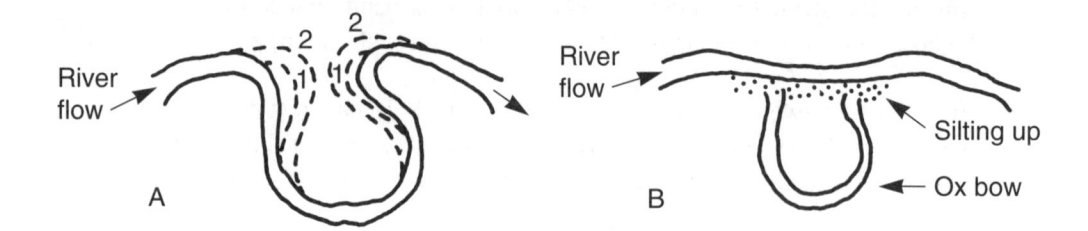

[Diagram A: meander neck being eroded at positions 1 and 2, with river flow arrows. Diagram B: ox bow lake formed with silting up along the new river course.]

Because the river flows more quickly on the outside of the bend, erosion through undercutting will take place there. This is seen in diagram A above where the neck of the meander is attacked from both outside bends to position 1, then to position 2. Then during a time of flood the river will break through, short circuiting the loop (diagram B). Silting will take place along the new river course so that the meander loop is permanently cut off, becoming an ox bow lake. **4**

2 COASTS

Question	Answer	Mark

1 (a)

> **Examiner's tip** Ensure that you match up the map and the aerial photograph accurately. Matching the railway routes and the tide on the photograph with High Water Mark will help you do this.

    (i)   X = Hoverport   Y = Richborough Power Station

    (ii) Ferry terminal; golf course; residential area; farmland.

    (iii) There is no sand or mud visible. **7**

(b)

> **Examiner's tip** Read Fig. 2 very carefully. If you do, you will find that together with Fig. 1 and the photograph you can answer all parts of (b) and (c) from the data supplied.

    (i)   1. They intend creating wildlife sanctuaries on the artificial islands.
          2. They intend to retain existing beaches.

    (ii) Hoverport

    (iii) To shelter the recreational basin from strong waves or severe weather.

    (iv) 1. It will be safer for dinghy sailing as it will be protected from the weather.

Answers to Unit 2

Question	Answer	Mark
	2. It will be possible to use the basin whatever the state of the tide.	6

(c)

Examiner's tip This is an example of the now well established type of question where you as a candidate are expected to put yourself into the mind of a third party, in this case a resident of Cliffsend. This should not be too difficult, as there is plenty of information in Fig. 2.

(i) 1. The new recreational/leisure facilities will be available to them if they become members.
2. New retail outlets will be built on their doorstep.
3. The beaches are guaranteed.
OR There will be less noise if the hoverport is removed.
OR Some employment openings may be created.

(ii) A big increase in traffic flow is likely so there will be more noise and air pollution.

4

(d)

Examiner's tip Here you will have to draw upon any case study of coastal pollution you have made. Note that the question uses the present and the past tense 'is' and 'has been'. So if you write about a situation that existed 5 or even 20 years ago, you will certainly satisfy the question's requirements. Again, there is no scale requirement. You could write about pollution in the Mediterranean or in a small British river estuary.

Named area = Croyde Bay, North Devon

This very attractive bay has had an increasingly serious problem during the past ten years or so. **Sewage** that is taken out to sea by pipeline is returned to the beach by waves and tides. The local sewage system is unable to cope with the increased load brought about by the vast increase in caravan/tenting holidays. In addition there has been a significant increase in **litter** pollution as gift shops and cafes have opened for the tourists. Some further pollution is brought here by longshore drift from the coast to the south while, occasionally, traces of **oil** pollution occur from ships cleaning out their tanks at sea. Finally, even the magnificent backing sand dunes have been defiled by damaging walking and the picking of unusual plant species.

(ii) There needs to be a modern sewage treatment plant which will return sewage to the sea in an almost clear liquid form. Given sufficient investment this could be done. Certainly the outfall pipe needs to be extended far out to sea so that the sewage is dispersed well away from the coast. For litter, more bins could be provided and/or penalties increased. The dunes have been fenced off with clear warning and explanatory notices to visitors.

8

Answers to Unit 3

3 WEATHERING AND GLACIATION

Question	Answer	Mark

1 (a)

> **Examiner's tip** Be sure to bring both photograph and map together in your mind. You must match the landforms on the two to determine the direction in which the camera was pointing. Look at the shape of the lake Red Tarn. The more irregular western edge of the lake on the map is top left on the photograph. Keppel Cove, which is NNW of Red Tarn on the map, is towards the top right of the photograph; that is the whole photograph is swivelled to the right, thus the camera was pointing north-west.

    (i)   A = Glenridding, B = Helvellyn, C = Striding Edge   3

    (ii)   C   1

> **Examiner's tip** Remember, an arête is a knife-edged ridge.

    (iii)   Thirlmere   1

(b) (i)   D = Biological   E = Chemical   F = Physical (or freeze/thaw)   3

> **Examiner's tip** Clearly, the examiner will be looking for three different processes.

    (ii)   Freeze/thaw   1

> **Examiner's tip** Remember that, though very cold, there was some melting during the day if the snow/ice surface faced the sun.

    (iii)   Scree

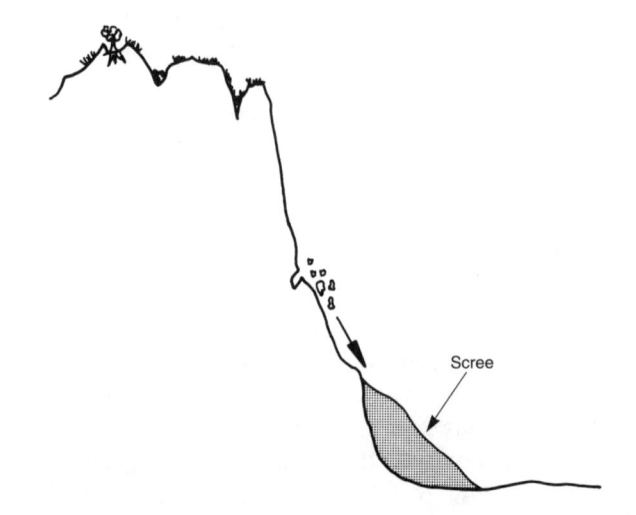

2

56

Answers to Unit 3

Question	Answer	Mark

(c) (i)

Examiner's tip — Three full descriptions of features are suggested for three marks.

The sides and back wall of the corrie are very steep and high, rising to over 900 m in places. These steep slopes are very rocky with some scree developments. The corrie is deepest in the centre, which has filled with water creating a lake.

3

(ii)

Examiner's tip — You are told to use at least one diagram. Make sure you do otherwise you will lose some marks. If you annotate the diagrams fully there is no need for separate text.

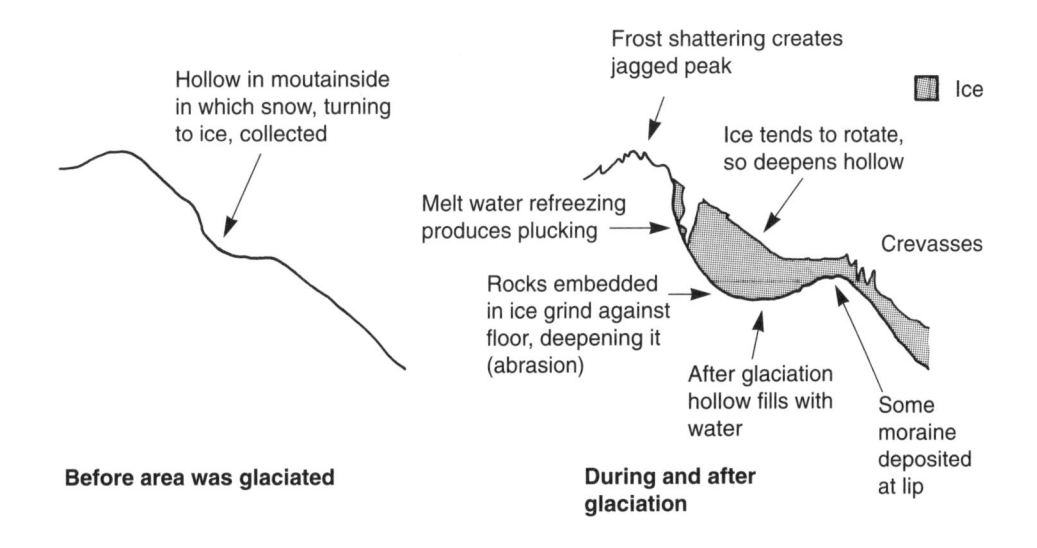

Diagram labels:
- Hollow in mountainside in which snow, turning to ice, collected
- Frost shattering creates jagged peak
- Ice
- Ice tends to rotate, so deepens hollow
- Melt water refreezing produces plucking
- Crevasses
- Rocks embedded in ice grind against floor, deepening it (abrasion)
- After glaciation hollow fills with water
- Some moraine deposited at lip

Before area was glaciated | **During and after glaciation**

6

(d)

Examiner's tip — The question states **at least** three reasons. Presumably, this means that a simple, undeveloped reason will gain one mark, a developed one up to two marks. So three full reasons or six bare reasons will give full marks. Below are five full reasons.

This region is popular with walkers all year round so the path surface and its original vegetation has little respite from walking boots. Once worn away the vegetation finds it difficult to regrow because:

- the prevailing low temperatures and harsh winds slow down growth,
- the poor soils, if not compacted by walkers, are eroded away by the heavy rainfall of the region,
- there is rapid runoff since some paths are on the knife-edge of ridges,
- freeze/thaw is rampant because at this height the temperature during the night is often below freezing and this helps to break up the paths.

6

Answers to Unit 3

Question	Answer	Mark
(ii)	Appeals can be made to walkers to redirect their steps. In severe cases of erosion walkers can be banned from the area. The ground may be covered with wire mesh to lessen the impact of feet and allow regeneration of vegetation. Water may be encouraged to move laterally through concrete grooving so reducing run off. Paths may be walled up to prevent their collapse.	4

4 WEATHER AND CLIMATE

Question	Answer	Mark

1 (a)

> **Examiner's tip** You are referred to a map showing the location of the world's equatorial rain forests and to four climate graphs.
> The world map includes latitude lines. These, clearly, are there to help you in your answers. The climate graphs show temperature and rainfall. Remember that on such graphs temperature is shown by a line, rainfall by columns. **Do not confuse them**. The graphs in this example are not printed on graph paper. So make sure, when making calculations, that you have a straight edge which you place absolutely horizontally to read the temperature and rainfall values from the scales. Again note that the height of these four stations above sea level is given. Pay attention to this. It does not matter too much in this question, but increased altitude means lower temperatures (1 °C lower for every 150 m of altitude) and often higher rainfall.

(i)	All the Equatorial Rain Forests are located within the Tropics. Most are located within 5° latitude of the Equator: in South America (the Amazon Basin), central Africa (the Congo Basin) and in south-east Asia.	3
(ii)	300 mm	1
(iii)	These are regions of high temperatures, so every day the heated ground heats the air above it. This rises, cools to condensation point, clouds form and heavy rain falls. (This is convectional rain.) Water vapour is added to the air through evaporation over the nearby seas before the air moves over the land. The luxuriant vegetation also adds lots of water vapour to the air through the process of transpiration.	3
(iv)	This is the difference in value between the highest and lowest mean monthly temperatures.	2
(v)	It is small because the Sun is **always** high in the sky and because night and day are equal in length throughout the year, so there is little variation in heat received.	2

Answers to Unit 4

Question	Answer	Mark
(b) (i)	Millibars	1

Examiner's tip This involves you in a study of a weather map. Some examination groups will give you a key for the symbols used on the map. Other groups will expect you to learn the symbols, and indeed may ask you questions that specifically test your knowledge of the symbols. Make sure that you are aware of the policy of your examination group.

(ii) An anticyclone or high — 1

(iii)

Examiner's tip A common error made by candidates is to confuse wind direction. Remember winds are named after the direction they blow **from** e.g. a south or southerly wind blows **from** the south.

(A) Isobars are far apart *OR* The pressure gradient is slack — 1

(B) Southern Britain has high pressure to the south-east and low pressure to the north-west. Winds blow around the high in a clockwise direction and slightly out, hence the southerly winds over southern Britain. — 3

(c)

Examiner's tip As with all questions when you have to read a passage, make sure you read it right through to gain an overview before you return to particular phrases or sentences that relate to specific questions. Also, note the date of the weather map; it is a **winter** chart.

(i) (A) Nitrogen dioxide — 1

(B) Asthma, coughing and other chest ailments — 1

(ii) The air is fairly still so there is no wind to disperse pollutants. Air in a winter high is stable and cold and is subsiding, so it traps pollutants near the ground. Air comes in from the nearby continent bringing in pollutants. — 2

(iii) Because cars are the main source of pollution such as nitrogen dioxide through their exhaust emissions. Alternative transport, such as train, tube or bus, creates much less air pollution in total as one engine carries many more passengers. — 4

2 (a)

Examiner's tip Once you have matched up the labels on the satellite image with their corresponding locations on the weather map, this question becomes a straightforward test of accurate symbol/isobaric map recognition.

Answers to Unit 4

Question	Answer	Mark

(i) A = Depression   B = Warm front   C = Cold front
D = Occlusion   E = Ridge

5

(ii)

> **Examiner's tip** Compare carefully the position of the black line (B) on the image and the warm front on the map. Remember a warm front has the main body of thick cloud **ahead** of its surface location.

The line runs through the Shetlands and eastern North Sea on the image but almost touches the north-east coast of Scotland and runs through the western North Sea on the map. The front on the image is ahead of the main body of cloud near the Shetlands.

2

(iii) Winds blow anticlockwise around a low so they blow from the east and north-east near F. Thus, clouds spiral round the centre of the low. (Technically the cloud is linked to a backbent occlusion.)

2

(iv) Temperature 4°C; 6 octas of cloud; rain shower; WNW wind; wind speed force 5 (or 23–27 knots); air pressure between 988 and 992 mb.

3

(v) Patchy white shadings denote shower clouds. It lies behind the cold front hence lower temperatures.

2

(b)

> **Examiner's tip** You must explain. Note the date – winter, and the time – night.

P = 5°C as it is fairly far south but in the middle of a ridge with clear skies and calm conditions. Has been dark for 9 or more hours so much nocturnal radiation. Chilled air has collected near the cold ground. There is no wind to disperse it so a temperature inversion occurs.

Q = 10°C because it is in the warm sector, and is therefore influenced by mild tropical maritime air. The cloud cover and strong winds prevent significant radiation.

R = 4°C because it is behind the cold front. The strong winds from the north-west quarter bring polar maritime air.

6

(c) (i)

> **Examiner's tip** You now have to compare two weather maps 24 hours apart. When studying the depression think of pressure, closeness of isobars, any directional movement of the centre or the fronts, and squeezing of the warm sector.

The depression has deepened greatly, the pressure at the centre falling from 972 to below 944 mb. As a result the isobars are now much closer together (the pressure gradient has steepened). The centre has moved more than 500 km to the north-east. Fronts have swept eastwards reducing the size of the cold sector.

4

Answers to Unit 5

Question	Answer	Mark

(ii)

Examiner's tip The map provides you with little information other than that the British Isles are in the cold sector of a depression with strong WNW or NW air flow – very strong over Scotland, least strong over south-east England, plus, of course, the fact that it is winter and 3 a.m. You must use your meteorological expertise. Use any two of the following three points.

Over most of the British Isles it is very windy, especially so in Scotland. This is because of the very steep pressure gradient, with about 50 mb difference in air pressure between Cornwall and the Shetlands.

There will be showers, as any polar maritime air mass will be unstable. Showers will be frequent over western coasts and hills as air is forced to rise.

Almost certainly the precipitation will be wintry over high ground, for temperatures fall with altitude at 1°C per 150 m, and this air mass is cold at this time of year.   **6**

5 POPULATION AND RESOURCES

Question	Answer	Mark

1 (a)

Examiner's tip The type of diagrams you are asked to study here are common in population questions. Remember that they show three features of the population: (i) its age structure, (ii) the male/female balance and (iii) the total size of the population.

(i) An official count of the population of a country. In Britain censuses are taken every ten years.   **1**

(ii) Both graphs are widest at the base and become progressively narrower as one moves up the age ranges. In short, they are both triangular and symmetrical.   **2**

Examiner's tip Note that the question states 'ways' so at least **two** similarities need to be mentioned.

(iii)

Examiner's tip There are three marks available so give three changes.

Answers to Unit 5

Question	Answer	Mark

The pyramid has changed from a triangular to a more pillar-like shape. The bulge in the middle shows that there were many more middle-aged people in 1988 than in 1891. The much wider top shows a big increase in the number of elderly people. The total population shown by the pyramid has increased considerably. **3**

(iv) The big increase in the number of people over 60 years of age means that:

- much more state money has to be spent on retirement pensions – hence moves to raise the pension age of women,

- more and more has to be spent on medical care in hospitals and nursing homes for the elderly,

- more welfare services such as 'homehelps' and 'meals on wheels' are needed.

All of this has to be provided by a working population between 20 and 60 years of age which forms a much smaller proportion of the total population than before – while many of this group are unemployed. Will they be able to continue paying towards pensions and medical services? **4**

(v)

> **Examiner's tip** Answers here can be based on religious objections, economic objections and on objections that population controls limit the rights of the individual.

Some people believe that controlling population growth is acting against God's will. The Roman Catholic church, for example, is opposed to artificial methods of contraception. Many more people are opposed to abortion, which they regard as tantamount to murder, while most people in this country disagree with infanticide, a measure which has been employed in China to control population numbers. Subsistence farmers in India are opposed to population controls as they need lots of children to work on their farms and to support them in their old age. **3**

(b) (i) Population density is the number of people per unit area. **1**

(ii) Bangladesh **1**

> **Examiner's tip** You need to study Fig. 4 to answer this question. It is not a very clear map. Make sure you find the correct column base before measuring the column's length.

(iii) Population density figures are more useful than total population figures as they tell you how crowded a country is. If you know about the country's economy, including whether farming or industry predominates, you can conclude whether it is overpopulated or underpopulated or neither. **2**

Answers to Unit 6

| Question | Answer | Mark |

(iv)

Examiner's tip This is the most important subquestion comprising almost one third of the total marks. Make sure you understand the word 'physical'. It is often taken to be those aspects of geography which are not 'human', e.g. relief, altitude, geology, soils and climate **but** this can vary. Check the syllabus for your exam on this matter. The command words 'comment on' are rather vague. Take them to mean 'write explanatory notes' on. Again, this question states 'with reference to places' so at least two must be chosen and named. Choose one sparsely and one densely populated area if you can.

Very few people live in Tibet because it is so high and inaccessible. Much of it is a high plateau over 3500 m above sea level, but there are deep valleys and raging rivers. This means that farming is very difficult. The high altitude leads to temperatures too low for crops to grow. Winds are often strong, so the thin soils are often blown away. Because Tibet is north of the Himalayas precipitation is low, again too low for successful farming, so the land has a low carrying capacity for humans and livestock. To build roads in this country is difficult and expensive. Steep slopes have to be overcome, bridges built and tunnels made. Roads can be blocked by fallen rocks. All this makes it unattractive for human settlement.

Not too far away from Tibet is the lower Ganges Valley. Here population density is very high. People have been attracted here because the land is low and flat so it is easy to farm and easy to build roads on. The low altitude leads to higher temperatures (over 20°C for much of the year), while every year the monsoon brings rain. This land is part of the Ganges flood plain, with soils which are alluvial and fertile. They are underlain by impermeable rock and will retain standing irrigation water. So this is an excellent region for growing rice, perhaps two crops a year. This will maintain a high density of population.

8

6 SETTLEMENT

| Question | Answer | Mark |

1 (a)

Examiner's tip The first part of this question asks you to study a model. Models are used a lot in geography, especially when studying the urban world. A model represents a perfect situation and is used to simplify reality. Real life situations can be very complex and difficult to understand but comparing them to a model allows us to see how they differ from the norm.

In this case you are asked to study a very common model in geography – the layout of a city in the developing world. Notice that the model contains a series of concentric rings (larger and larger circles) with a number of sectors. The smallest circle usually identifies the city centre. Take special note that this is a city in a **developing** country. Cities in the developed world differ in a number of ways.

Answers to Unit 6

Question	Answer	Mark

(i)

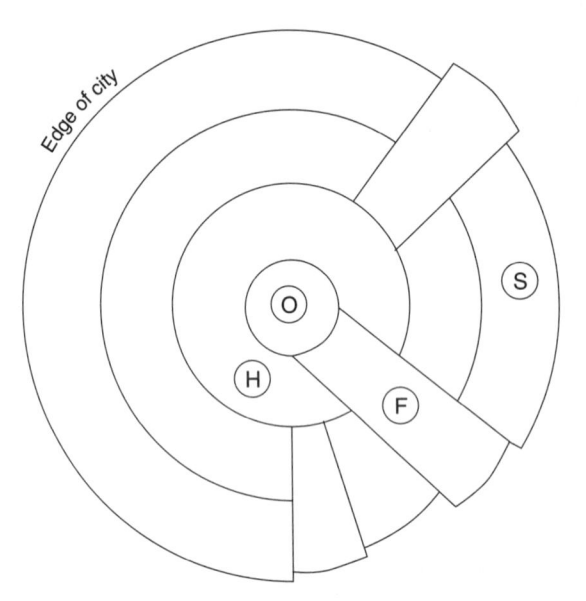

4

(ii) Many families have nowhere else to live – their only other option is the street. They have very low incomes and cannot afford to buy or rent a permanent dwelling. They use what is available to build a shelter.   2

(iii) Land is very expensive as the Central Business District is the most accessible part of the city. High rise buildings use only a relatively small piece of land. Many businesses want to locate there so there is competition for land, as it is scarce. High rise buildings allow more office space to be created.   2

(b)

> **Examiner's tip** Here there is a clear instruction to 'use map evidence only' so that is what you must do. Read the question to see which part of the map you must refer to and then study the map carefully. Note that there are three marks available so you must mention three things – but you are asked to say something about the site of Keswick **and** why it has grown.

(i) Situated on gentle sloping land away from the river's flood plain, Keswick lies at a narrow section of a west–east route through the mountains. The gap through the mountains is a natural route focus for roads and formerly, the railway. The presence of many campsites suggest that this area is a major tourist centre and Keswick has grown to accommodate them.   3

(ii) Road traffic has increased tremendously over the past 20 years, especially lorries. The closure of the railway line has also added to road traffic. Keswick's narrow streets become easily congested. Keswick attracts many more tourists as people's leisure time increases, thus adding to the congestion.   2

Answers to Unit 6

Question	Answer	Mark
(iii)	Answer = 4.25 km	1

Examiner's tip Here you are asked to measure a distance. As the distance to be measured is not direct you must split the distance up into a series of straight lines. The best way of doing this is to use the edge of a piece of paper. Lay your completed length of paper against the linear scale. Make sure you give your answer in kilometres.

(iv)

Examiner's tip Make sure you state at the beginning of each answer whether they will be for or against the by-pass.

A retired couple living in Keswick – For the by-pass. It will reduce the amount of traffic going through the town centre which will in turn cut down the amount of noise and pollution and make it safer for pedestrians and shoppers.

A shopkeeper in Keswick – Against the by-pass. It will cut down the number of people travelling through the town centre reducing the amount of passing trade. His profits may well fall.

A farmer – Against the by-pass. He will lose some of his land. His farm may be divided in two making it difficult to get from one side to the other. The noise and fumes from the traffic may affect his animals. **3**

(v) Introduce a one-way system. Install part-time traffic lights at roundabouts and major junctions which operate during peak traffic flow times. Have a priority flow scheme which caters for incoming traffic during the morning rush hour and outgoing traffic during the evening rush hour. **3**

(c)

Examiner's tip Here you are asked to study two maps of the same place at different times. Look at them closely to gain an overview before looking at the questions. Notice the different scale of these maps compared to the OS map – here the scale is much larger. Note any changes you observe.

(i) Dormitory or commuter village **1**

(ii) More large, detached houses and more Local Authority (council) housing *OR* more bungalows. **2**

(iii)

Examiner's tip Your answers here must come from Fig. 2 as you are directed to it.

Answers to Unit 6

Question	Answer	Mark
	Large camp site and caravan site now present. A hotel and a motel have been built.	2

7 AGRICULTURE – SPECIFICALLY DAIRYING

Question	Answer	Mark

1

> **Examiner's tip** The map links rainfall with the quantity of dairy cattle kept. The lines on the map are isohyets – lines joining places of the same rainfall total over a period of time, in this case the month of July. Study the key and look for any trends – notice the higher the July rainfall, the greater the percentage of dairy cattle.

(a) (i) The further south and east, the lower the percentage of livestock which are dairy cattle. — 1

(ii) The drier it is, the lower the percentage of livestock that are dairy cattle. — 1

(iii)

> **Examiner's tip** Think of the way in which the climate of southern Europe affects the grass eaten by dairy cows, the cows themselves and the milk they produce.

Too dry – very little grass grows so there is not enough for the cattle to eat. What grass there is lacks moisture (not lush) so little is turned into milk.

Too hot – cows perspire so lose moisture, little milk produced per cow, uneconomic. The hot climate means milk is difficult to store/transport as it goes off quickly. — 2

(b) (i)

> **Examiner's tip** The question asks for one **full** reason so you must extend your answer to gain the full two marks.

Close to the farmhouse so cows can be brought to the milking parlour quickly and easily.
OR On higher ground so the drainage is good. — 2

(ii)

> **Examiner's tip** Study the contour lines paying particular attention to the height of each contour.

Underline uphill then downhill — 1

Answers to Unit 7

Question	Answer	Mark
(iii)	1. Answer = 4.5 km	1

Examiner's tip The best technique to use is the edge of a piece of paper. Measure in a series of straight lines and then use the key to convert to kilometres.

	2. The field is a long way from the farm so the farmer could waste time getting there. He could use a lot of fuel in getting machinery to the field so increasing his costs. OR Too far to take his livestock to on a regular basis, as cattle become tired.	2
(iv)	1. Permanent pasture is a field of grass that is never ploughed up. The field is not used for any other crop.	1
	2. Some of it is close to the farm and is used for grazing the farmer's milk herd as it is not far to bring the cows in for milking. The fields furthest away from the farmhouse, are poorly drained as a result of being close to the valley floor (boggy for much of the year) and are therefore, unsuitable to grow any other crop.	2

Examiner's tip There are two areas of permanent pasture on this farm. Both areas must be mentioned in order to gain the full two marks.

(v)	As part of a crop rotation system which enables him to maintain the fertility of his soil. To sell crops as well as milk to supplement his income. In that way he safeguards some income if a crop fails or his dairy herd becomes diseased. OR Much of the grain can be used as a fodder crop – one which is fed to animals during winter.	4
(c) (i)	A limit on the amount of milk that can be produced.	1
(ii)	Over-production by European farmers had created a large stockpile of dairy produce (a 'butter mountain') so there was no demand for the milk produced.	2
(iii)	Herds of dairy cattle were too large so many cattle have had to be destroyed. During the 1960s and 70s farmers were encouraged to borrow money to increase stock/increase the size of their farm/invest in new machinery. They are now faced with large interest payments that cannot be met. They may have to look for alternative uses for their land – diversification, e.g. pick-your-own fruit, farm shop, pony trekking, camping, tourism. They may be forced to sell off parts of the farm to, for example, property developers or for golf courses.	4
(d)		

Examiner's tip Here you are given a choice. Your answer can either concentrate on one way, in which case an extensive answer is needed, OR you could mention several ways in less detail like the ones given below. You do not have to use one of the examples given.

Answers to Unit 7

Question	Answer	Mark

Organic farming – the excessive use of artificial fertilizers has become an environmentally sensitive issue. Increased consumer choice has created a demand for natural produce. It is more expensive to produce and, therefore, costs more in shops but some people are prepared to pay the higher prices.

Set-aside scheme – this is where the farmer is paid by the government to take land out of production. Farmers have been producing too much food in recent years and so subsidies are offered to let land remain unproductive and so revert back to nature, or to plant woodland.

Replanting of hedgerows – modern farm practices require large machines which work best in large fields. There has been a tendency for every available piece of land to be used to maximize profits. This has meant digging up hedgerows. Hedgerows not only act as field boundaries but their roots bind the soil together, which helps prevent soil erosion, and they are a home for many species of wildlife. Government subsidies have been available for those farmers who wish to re-establish the hedgerows on their farm.

6

8 MANUFACTURING INDUSTRY

Question	Answer	Mark

1 (a)

Examiner's tip — Here you are asked to study a systems diagram of iron and steel manufacture. You must be sure of the meaning of the words at the top of each column. Your task is to place each of nine terms under the correct heading. As you fill in your answers, cross off the ones you have used. Use each word only once and do not make up your own. Take special note of the 'inputs' section. Two of the missing inputs are raw materials. These raw materials have to be written on the second and third lines down, as indicated by the brackets.

Answer in this order:

Inputs = capital, iron ore, coking coal, skilled workforce, electricity
Processes = steel mill
Outputs = steel sheets
Markets = shipbuilding, car industry

9

(b)

Examiner's tip — The diagram itself does not help you to answer the question – it is the words in the boxes that are important. Do not write in the boxes. You are given a choice. There are eight boxes and you have to write about any five of them. Think carefully about each factor before committing yourself to answer. Make sure your answer refers to specific industries as this is stated in the question. Read the example given – it is there to help you – notice that it mentions three separate industries. Make sure you state which factor you are referring to at the beginning of each section and how it influences the **location** of the factory. As there are nine marks for this section assume each factor is worth about two.

Answers to Unit 8

Question	Answer	Mark

Markets – A location near the main market cuts transport costs. In the case of large industries such as steel making, the market can be worldwide, with steel being exported to countries all over the world. As steel has a low value/bulk ratio a location near a port is desirable. Smaller factories, such as a small bakery, may have only a small, local market. A location in a town is desirable.

Raw materials – Raw materials can be heavy, bulky and costly to transport. Therefore, a location close to the source of the raw materials is desirable, e.g. a cement works may look to locate near a limestone quarry. If large amounts of raw materials have to be imported a coastal location is desirable, e.g. ICI's petrochemical works on Teesside receives its raw material, oil, direct by pipeline from the North Sea.

Labour – Some industries, such as hi-tech industries, require a highly trained, skilled workforce. A location close to training establishments and universities for research purposes is desirable. Other factories require a large pool of unskilled workers. A location near major urban areas would be essential.

Transport – Transport is essential for all factories to bring raw materials in and take finished products out. The cheapest form of transport for heavy, bulky products is water, e.g. crude oil is transported by large, ocean-going super tankers and oil refineries are located near deep water ports. For lighter goods, which travel shorter distances, road transport is more important. Easy access to a motorway is essential.

Power – During the last century, as the only sources of power were coal or water, all industry was forced to locate on the coalfields (such as the iron and steel industry) or close to fast-flowing streams (such as wool mills). Nowadays power is easily transported in the form of electricity so, in developed countries, power is no longer such an important consideration. However, in many developing countries it still remains an important factor in determining industrial location. **9**

(c)

> **Examiner's tip** Here you are asked to study a flow diagram. Each statement in the boxes has a knock-on effect. Follow the arrows to find the sequence of events. You are given a wide choice of area; indeed it does not even have to be in the UK. You can choose an area where industry has declined, such as the old coalfield areas of Britain, or an area of industrial growth, such as along the M4 corridor. Make sure you read each side of the diagram before deciding which route to take. Make sure that you know a relevant case study – an inappropriate choice can make answering the question impossible. You must specify the area and say whether it is an area of growth or an area of decline.

Derby, an area of growth

(i) In the mid 1980s, Toyota, the Japanese car manufacturer, decided to build a new car plant near Derby. After fierce competition from

Answers to Unit 8

Question	Answer	Mark

Humberside and south Wales, the 280 acre, greenfield site at Burnaston was chosen ahead of nine other sites. It was hoped that the £700 million factory would employ up to 3000 workers and produce 200 000 new cars annually.

(ii) As a result of trade restrictions on the import of Japanese cars, Toyota had been looking for a European production base. Derby was chosen because: (i) a good transport network ensured easy access to national and international markets; (ii) a multi-skilled workforce was available; (iii) there were training and research establishments nearby; (iv) other internationally renowned firms, such as Rolls Royce, were already successfully established in the Derby area; (v) the site offered plenty of room for expansion; (vi) financial support was available from Derbyshire County Council.

(iii) Employment was created at a time when local industry was in recession. As well as jobs in the factory itself, up to 3000 other jobs were created in associated industries – as well as jobs in construction during the building phase. Improvements in the local infrastructure, with new roads and railways, along with a higher profile and growing reputation, attracted other firms to Derby. Socially, people were much better off. As incomes rose, people became wealthier and so demanded more services. Local taxes were paid so the Councils had more money for the upkeep of roads and schools. House prices rose as more people moved into the area.

(iv) Being a greenfield site, the building of the factory replaced prime agricultural land. The building of more road and rail links also destroyed the natural environment and wildlife habitats. More traffic on the roads, especially car transporters, increased congestion and lead to more noise and other forms of pollution. Burnaston House, a listed building of architectural importance, is now surrounded by a modern factory. **12**

9 RETAILING

Question	Answer	Mark

1

Examiner's tip — Note the scale of this map is 1:25 000, i.e. 4 cm = 1 km. Compare it to other OS maps in this book. You should familiarize yourself with all types.

(a) (i) Any three from: hospital, school, swimming pool, information centre, museum, hotel, mountain rescue post, telephone, public convenience, Town Hall, parking, railway station, library, Post Office. **3**

Answers to Unit 9

Question	Answer	Mark

(ii)

Examiner's tip A sharp rise in difficulty. Here you must use map evidence to **explain** why Settle has become the largest settlement in the area.

It is a bridging point, being an important routeway across the River Ribble. It is a route centre as many of the roads in the area lead to Settle. The land is gently sloping and lower than much of the surrounding land so there is room for the town to grow.

3

(iii)

Examiner's tip This is not a typical example of superstore location. You have to remember that Settle is a relatively small settlement in a rural area so the usual rules of superstore location may not apply. In this case, the **site** means the location of the plot of ground on which the superstore is to be built.

The site is an area of flat land close to the town centre. There is housing nearby and it is also close to a road and a car park.

3

(b) (i)

Examiner's tip There are five segments which make up your completed bar. Be careful, accuracy is important.

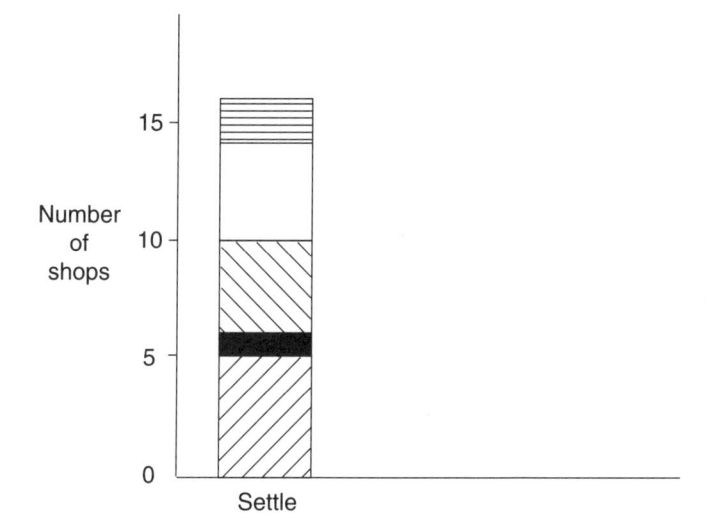

3

(ii) Settle has the largest number and greatest variety of shops. Shops selling high order goods are only found in Settle. The other three settlements have low order shops only. Three of the four settlements have a Post Office.

3

Answers to Unit 9

Question	Answer	Mark

(iii)

Examiner's tip Make sure you say something about both gift shops and electrical shops.

Gift shops provide a service for tourists. They are located in the most accessible place. Settle is the easiest place to visit so is likely to have the most tourists. Electrical shops sell high order goods. They are goods that are bought infrequently. These shops need a larger number of people to support them so they are located in the largest settlement.   **2**

(iv)

Examiner's tip This question tests your knowledge of how shopping patterns have changed in recent years.

There would probably have been more shops in each of the surrounding villages offering a greater variety of services. Settle has increased in importance as a tourist centre in recent years so there may well have been fewer gift shops in Settle twenty years ago.   **2**

(c) (i)

Examiner's tip An explanation of geographical terms is required here.

The **threshold** is the number of customers needed to support a particular shop. The **range** is the distance people are prepared to travel in order to purchase goods in a particular shop. The higher the order of goods sold (the more luxury the items), the larger the threshold has to be and the greater the range.   **3**

Examiner's tip The remaining two parts of this question approach the topic of superstore versus corner shop from a different perspective than is usual. They are looking at the shortcomings of the superstore rather than its strengths.

(ii) The personal relationship and sense of community offered by a small shop would not be available in a superstore. There may be less of a service offered by the superstore, for example, no home delivery available.   **2**

(d) Superstores offer a greater variety of goods at cheaper prices. Local shops would not be able to compete and may close. Customers may have to travel further in order to shop. This may be a problem for people who have no transport, especially the elderly. Shop workers may lose their jobs and have to seek work elsewhere. This could begin a trend of decline.   **6**

Answers to Unit 10

10 TOURISM AND LEISURE

Question	Answer	Mark

1

Examiner's tip This question requires you to have a lot of specialized knowledge. The topics cover quite a range so thorough revision is essential. In order to answer the question in full you need knowledge of the geography and climate of Europe and North Africa, some understanding of glacial and limestone landforms, a knowledge of National Parks and a complete understanding of the effects tourists have in National Parks and in developing countries as well as a detailed knowledge of winter tourism.

(i)

Examiner's tip Here you are asked to read a lot of information before attempting the question. Whilst reading each postcard carefully try to gain an impression of the type of holiday being described. The map you are given is not very detailed so think carefully before putting in your letters.

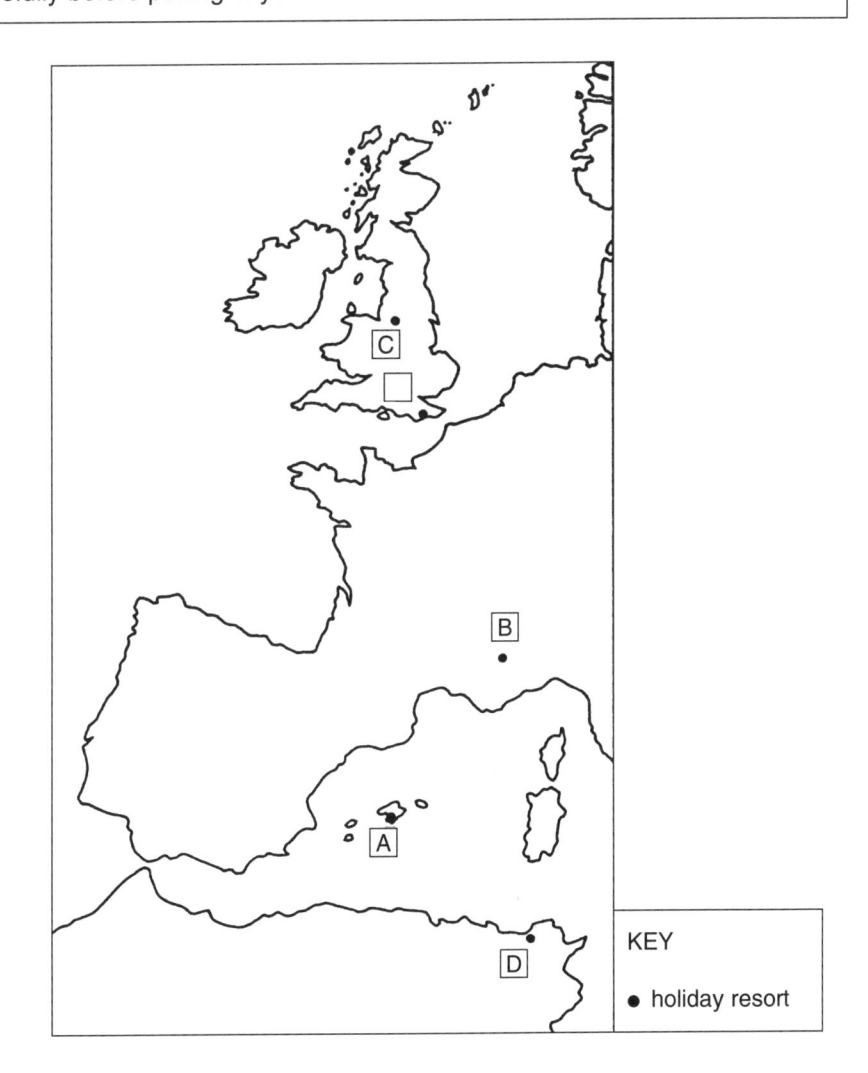

4

Answers to Unit 10

Question	Answer	Mark
(ii)		

Examiner's tip Make sure you identify which of the two features you are describing.

	A corrie is a feature of glacial erosion. It is an 'armchair'-like feature with steep back and side walls. Its open side faces a valley and there is sometimes a lake in the bottom of the corrie.	2
(iii)	Pot-holes are a feature of limestone scenery as rainwater dissolves the rock removing it in solution. Soil does not form in limestone areas so bare grey-white rock outcrops are common.	2
(iv)	National Parks were set up to protect and enhance areas of 'outstanding natural beauty'.	2
(v)	Tourists may trample over farm land, leaving gates open, leaving litter behind and worrying farm animals. Noise and air pollution could disturb local residents and increased traffic could lead to congested roads, especially in summer.	2
(vi)		

Examiner's tip You must name specific places in your answer, preferably ones you have studied in detail. Make sure you mention advantages as well as disadvantages.

	In recent years many people have been attracted to Kenya for safari-type holidays. Kenyans have benefited through the creation of many jobs such as hotel staff, tour guides and drivers; tourists spending money in the local markets buying souvenirs; the money gained from touring big game reserves can go towards the upkeep and maintenance of animals. The disadvantages are that the money raised from tourism goes to tour operators or a few wealthy businessmen, it is not spread evenly throughout the country so not everyone benefits; tourists draw on limited local resources of water, electricity and fuel; local customs and traditions may suffer through the need to pamper tourists.	
	Upland farming areas of Britain, such as mid Wales, benefit from tourists in summer. Farming incomes are supplemented by providing bed and breakfast accommodation or selling local produce in farm shops and/or by offering guided walks and nature trails. The disadvantages are that tourists may trample on farmers' land, destroying crops and worrying animals, and that more tourists lead to congested roads and more litter.	6
(b)	The cold winter temperatures and adequate supply of precipitation provide excellent snow conditions attracting tourists for winter sports. Total precipitation is lower than many parts of the UK so the warm summers attract hikers and those who enjoy mountain scenery.	3

Answers to Unit 11

Question	Answer	Mark

(c)

Examiner's tip Study both the photograph and the diagram carefully. The key to the diagram can be most useful. Take special note of the direction of the north line. You must mention both natural and man-made attractions.

(i) Natural – It is a mountain environment with a plentiful supply of snow. Sunny days and clear blue skies make it ideal for skiing. There are a range of ski slopes catering for beginners and the more advanced skier. Ski runs are on north-facing slopes reducing the risk of snow melt.

Man-made – Many apartments and hotels have been built for accommodation. Facilities for children are provided, such as a crêche and a kindergarten, and ski hire and tuition. Prepared skiing areas (pistes) and a network of interconnecting ski lifts are available. **6**

(ii) The mountain environment is delicately balanced and thousands of visitors can upset sensitive plant and animal habitats. Removal of trees for ski runs leads to greater soil erosion in spring and increases the risk of avalanche in winter. The risk of flooding can increase as (i) bulldozing ski runs compacts the soil, reducing infiltration rates and (ii) tarmac car parking areas increase surface runoff. Small mountain streams can become raging torrents. **3**

11 EMPLOYMENT STRUCTURES IN DEVELOPED AND DEVELOPING COUNTRIES

Question	Answer	Mark

1 (a) (i) 1. The primary sector contains those industries which extract products from the Earth's surface.
2. The secondary sector is made up of industries in which raw materials are put together to create something that people want. **2**

(ii)

Examiner's tip You will need to examine these pie charts closely because some of the countries in the table have similar employment structures.

1 = United Kingdom   2 = Brazil **2**

Answers to Unit 11

Question	Answer	Mark

(iii)

Examiner's tip Note that the two axes concern primary and tertiary only; so you are matching these two components up. Thus, in A countries 1 and 2 will have high primary (>50) and low tertiary (<50) percentages.

A = India	B = Brazil	C = United Kingdom
Ghana	South Korea	Australia

3

(iv) Developing = A   Developed = C   N.I.C. = B   1

(v)

Examiner's tip A wide range of characteristics can be used to answer this question. Choose any two of the following examples.

1. High birth rate, lowering death rate so high net reproduction.
2. Low gross national product.
OR Poorly developed communication network.
Poorly established welfare and social services.

2

(b)

Examiner's tip Study the data provided very carefully. You are given a lot of information, some of which can be used directly when answering the subsequent questions.

(i)

Examiner's tip Do not forget the shading when completing this bar graph.

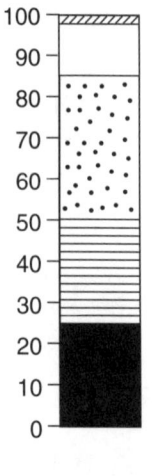

2

(ii) 1. Imports restricted   2. Cheap loans or tax incentives   2

(iii) Primary   1

Answers to Unit 11

Question	Answer	Mark

(iv)

Examiner's tip The changes you have to explain are the decline in the primary sector and the increases in the secondary and tertiary sectors. The chart provides you with strong clues for these changes but you are also expected to draw upon your own knowledge.

1. The introduction of machinery into mining and farming meant fewer workers were needed in the primary sector, forcing them to move into the secondary and tertiary sectors.
2. The government restricted imports forcing manufacturing to develop. *OR* Multinational (transnational) companies moved into the country with massive investment in the secondary sector.

4

(v) 1. Clothing is an essential, so there is a large home market in all developing countries for textiles.
2. The textile industry is fairly labour intensive. Labour in these countries is cheap. Thus costs of production are relatively low.
OR Most developing countries are tropical, so they grow cotton. This reduces costs.

4

(vi)

Examiner's tip Note the use of the words 'economic' and 'social'. Economic relates to business and industry, social to people's well being, for example working hours, health and education.

Economic – Multinational companies may take their profits out of the country and invest them elsewhere.
OR The massive loans taken out to finance industrialization may cripple the country's economy.

Social – Many employees have to work very long hours.
OR Urbanization has led to growth of squatter settlements.

4

(c)

Examiner's tip This is a very open question. You can tackle industry or agriculture in any area of the developed or developing world. What you must do is specify the area and discuss decline.

Name of area: South-east Lancashire including what is now Greater Manchester.

(i) **Industry**. In the nineteenth century this was **the** most important **cotton textile** area in the world. It declined in the twentieth century because:

- Lancashire could no longer rely on cheap imports of raw cotton from developing countries.

- Lancashire could not compete with imports of cloth from developing countries, such as India, where overheads were much lower.

Answers to Unit 11

Question	Answer	Mark

- Lancashire mills were slow to modernize their equipment.

- synthetic fibres, such as nylon, reduced the market for cotton cloth.

(ii) There was a big rise in unemployment. This was very serious for male workers as there were few alternatives in an area where coal mining and heavy engineering were also in recession. There was a cumulative run down in facilities as people in the area had less and less money to spend. Many people moved away from the area in search of work. In some towns in the area, where employment for women still existed, they became the chief earners. **9**

2

Examiner's tip This is a scattergraph which shows the relationship between life expectancy and the percentage of the workforce employed in agriculture. Working in agriculture occupies the horizontal axis because it is thought to have an effect on life expectancy.

(a) The lower the percentage of the workforce employed in agriculture, the higher the life expectancy. **2**

(b) (i) If life expectancy is low, it suggests poor nutrition, poor medical services, high infant mortality and possibly people living in shanty towns; all indicative of a developing poor country.

(ii) As a country develops, so the percentage employed in agriculture declines. Agriculture becomes highly mechanized and employs less and less labour. So the lower the agricultural workforce percentage, the higher the stage of development. **4**